First World War
and Army of Occupation
War Diary
France, Belgium and Germany

60 DIVISION
179 Infantry Brigade
London Regiment
2/15 Battalion
4 January 1915 - 30 November 1916

WO95/3030/5

The Naval & Military Press Ltd
www.nmarchive.com
Published in association with The National Archives

Published by

The Naval & Military Press Ltd

Unit 10 Ridgewood Industrial Park,

Uckfield, East Sussex,

TN22 5QE England

Tel: +44 (0) 1825 749494

www.naval-military-press.com

www.nmarchive.com

This diary has been reprinted in facsimile from the original. Any imperfections are inevitably reproduced and the quality may fall short of modern type and cartographic standards.

© **Crown Copyright**
Images reproduced by permission of The National Archives, London, England, 2015.

Contents

Document type	Place/Title	Date From	Date To
Heading	WO95/3030/5		
Heading	60 Division 179 Brigade 2/15 London Regt (Civil Service Rifles) 1915 Jan-1916 Jun		
War Diary	White City London	04/01/1915	24/01/1915
War Diary	Dorking	26/01/1915	30/01/1915
Heading	2/15th Battn. London Regt. Dorking War Diary 1st To 28th Feby (m) 1915		
War Diary	Dorking	01/02/1915	21/02/1915
War Diary	London	22/02/1915	28/02/1915
War Diary	Dorking	01/03/1915	10/03/1915
War Diary	Sandwich	11/03/1915	11/03/1915
War Diary	Dorking	12/03/1915	29/03/1915
War Diary	Watford	30/03/1915	16/05/1915
War Diary	Ford Field	17/05/1915	18/05/1915
War Diary	Watford	18/05/1915	18/05/1915
War Diary	Fort Bishop's Hatfield	19/05/1915	19/05/1915
War Diary	Saffron Walden	20/05/1915	31/05/1915
War Diary	Saffron Walden	01/06/1915	31/08/1915
Heading	War Diary Of The 2/15th Battn. London Regt. 1 Sept 1915 To 30 Sept 1915 Volume 1		
War Diary	Saffron Walden	02/09/1915	05/10/1915
War Diary	Stebbing	06/10/1915	06/10/1915
War Diary	Braintree	06/10/1915	07/10/1915
War Diary	Stebbing	07/10/1915	08/10/1915
War Diary	Saffron Walden	08/10/1915	26/10/1915
War Diary	Bishops Stortford	27/10/1915	28/11/1915
War Diary	Ware	29/11/1915	30/11/1915
War Diary	War Diary Of The 2/15th Battalion London Regiment From 1st December 1915 To 31st December 1915		
War Diary	Ware	01/12/1915	31/12/1915
Miscellaneous	Appendix A Brigade Concentration March 6 December 1915		
Miscellaneous	2/15th Battn. London Regiment.	06/12/1915	06/12/1915
Miscellaneous	2/15th Battalion London Regiment	06/12/1915	06/12/1915
Heading	Appendix B. Battalion Concentration March By Light		
Miscellaneous	2/15th Battalion, London Regiment	10/12/1915	10/12/1915
Heading	Appendix C		
Miscellaneous	2/15th Battalion London Regiment	15/12/1915	15/12/1915
Heading	Appendix D Officers Tactical Exercise 22 Dec 1915		
Miscellaneous	2/15th Battalion London Regiment		
Heading	War Diary Of The 2/15th Battalion London Regiment From 1 January 1916 To 31 January 1916 (Volume 2)		
War Diary	Ware	01/01/1916	22/01/1916
War Diary	Warminster	22/01/1916	22/01/1916
War Diary	Longbridge Deverill	23/01/1916	31/01/1916
Heading	Appendix I Tactical Exercise For Offers. 5th/4th Jany 1916		
Miscellaneous	2/15th Battalion, London Regt.	05/01/1916	05/01/1916
Heading	Appendix II Report Of Month Of Tactical Scheme 7 January 1916		

Miscellaneous	2/15th Battalion London Regt.	07/01/1916	07/01/1916
Heading	Appendix III Tactical Exercise 1 12 Jany 1916. Scheme And Spiral Idea		
Miscellaneous	2/15th Battalion London Regiment	12/01/1916	12/01/1916
Miscellaneous	2/15th Battalion London Regt.	12/01/1916	12/01/1916
Heading	Appendix IV		
Miscellaneous	2/15th Battalion London Regiment.	19/01/1916	19/01/1916
Heading	War Diary Of The 2/15th Battalion London Regiment 1 February 1916 To 29 February 1916		
War Diary	Longbridge Deverill	01/02/1916	29/02/1916
Heading	War Diary Of The 2/15th Battalion London Regt. From 1 March 1916 To 31 March 1916 (Volume 2)		
War Diary	Longbridge Deverill	01/03/1916	31/03/1916
Miscellaneous	Appendix I		
Miscellaneous	2/15th Battalion London Regiment		
Miscellaneous	Secret.		
Miscellaneous	Memorandum	07/03/1916	07/03/1916
Miscellaneous	Return Of Casualties Operations On 6th. March	06/03/1916	06/03/1916
Heading	War Diary Of The 2/15th Battalion London Regiment From 1 April 1916 To 30 April 1916 (Volume 2)		
War Diary	Longbridge Deverill	01/04/1916	29/04/1916
War Diary	Neyland	29/04/1916	30/04/1916
Heading	War Diary Of The 2/15th Battalion London Regt. From 1 May To 31 May 1916 (Volume 2)		
War Diary	Neyland	01/05/1916	01/05/1916
War Diary	Queens Town	02/05/1916	02/05/1916
War Diary	Neyland Fotay	03/05/1916	06/05/1916
War Diary	Ballincollig	06/05/1916	07/05/1916
War Diary	Coachford	08/05/1916	08/05/1916
War Diary	Macrooma	08/05/1916	11/05/1916
War Diary	Mill Street	11/05/1916	11/05/1916
War Diary	Rosslare	12/05/1916	12/05/1916
War Diary	Fishguard	12/05/1916	12/05/1916
War Diary	Warminster	13/05/1916	13/05/1916
War Diary	Longbridge Deverill	14/05/1916	31/05/1916
Heading	War Diary Of The 2/15th Battalion London Regt. From 1 June To 29 June 1916 (Volume)		
War Diary	Longbridge Deverill	01/06/1916	21/06/1916
War Diary	War Diary Of The 2/15th Battn London Regiment From 22 June 1916 To 30 June 1916 (Volume 2)		
War Diary	Longbridge Deverill	22/06/1916	22/06/1916
War Diary	Warminster	22/06/1916	22/06/1916
War Diary	Southampton	22/06/1916	22/06/1916
War Diary	Havre	23/06/1916	24/06/1916
War Diary	Penin	25/06/1916	25/06/1916
War Diary	Maroeuil	26/06/1916	30/06/1916
Heading	Divisional Tactical Exercise May 26th, 1916. 179th Brigade Operation Orders By Col E.W. Baird, Commanding.		
Miscellaneous	179th Infantry Brigade Orders By Colonel E.W. Baird. Commanding.	26/05/1916	26/05/1916
Heading	60th Division 179th Infy Bde 2-15th Bn London Regt 1915 Jan-1916 Nov		
Heading	War Diary Of The 2/15th Battn London Regt. From 1 July 1916 To 31 July 1916		
War Diary	Trenches	01/07/1916	05/07/1916

War Diary	Neuville St Vast	05/07/1916	13/07/1916
War Diary	Bray	13/07/1916	16/07/1916
War Diary	Subsector I	17/07/1916	31/07/1916
Heading	War Diary Of The 2/15th Battn London Regiment From 1 August 1916 To 31 August 1916 (Volume 2)		
War Diary	Subsector I	01/08/1916	09/08/1916
War Diary	Rest Billets	10/08/1916	17/08/1916
War Diary	Subsector	18/08/1916	31/08/1916
Heading	War Diary Of 2/15th London Regt From 1 Sept 1916 to 30 Sept 1916 (Volume 2)		
War Diary	Sub Sector I	01/09/1916	01/09/1916
War Diary	Rest Billets	01/09/1916	08/09/1916
War Diary	Subsector 1 Centre 1	09/09/1916	24/09/1916
War Diary	Rest Billets	25/09/1916	30/09/1916
Miscellaneous	Appendix I G.O.C. XVII CORPS.	11/09/1915	11/09/1915
Miscellaneous	Appendix II Statement by Lieut. B. Peatfield.	11/09/1916	11/09/1916
Miscellaneous	Statement By 2nd Lieut Thompson	11/09/1916	11/09/1916
Miscellaneous	Appendix III Extract From 60th Divisional Orders dated 15th September, 1916.	15/09/1916	15/09/1916
Miscellaneous	Appendix IV Extract From 60th Divisional Orders dated 21st Sept. 1916.	21/09/1916	21/09/1916
Heading	War Diary Of 2/15th Battn London Regiment From 1 Oct 1916 To 31 Oct 1916 (Volume 2)		
War Diary	Subsector Centre	01/10/1916	18/10/1916
War Diary	Rest Billets	19/10/1916	22/10/1916
War Diary	Hermaville Tilloy	23/10/1916	23/10/1916
War Diary	Sericourt & Honval	24/10/1916	28/10/1916
War Diary	Bealcourt	28/10/1916	29/10/1916
War Diary	Lanches	29/10/1916	31/10/1916
Heading	War Diary Of The 2/15th Battn London Regt. From 1 Nov To 30 Nov 1916 (Volume 2)		
War Diary	Lanches	01/11/1916	02/11/1916
War Diary	Francieres	03/11/1916	14/11/1916
War Diary	Loncpre	15/11/1916	15/11/1916
War Diary	Francieres	15/11/1916	16/11/1916
War Diary	Marseilles	17/11/1916	28/11/1916
War Diary	Salonika	28/11/1916	30/11/1916

WO 95/3030/5

60 DIVISION

179 BRIGADE

2/15 LONDON REGT
(CIVIL SERVICE RIFLES)

1915 JAN — 1916 JUN

2902

Army Form C. 2118.

2/5 Lond
2/5 Lond...

WAR DIARY
or
INTELLIGENCE SUMMARY.
(Erase heading not required.)

Instructions regarding War Diaries and Intelligence Summaries are contained in F.S. Regs., Part II. and the Staff Manual respectively. Title pages will be prepared in manuscript.

Hour, Date, Place	Summary of Events and Information	Remarks and references to Appendices
6.30 a.m. 4th January 1915 WHITE CITY, LONDON.	The Battalion left the White City in two parties, entraining at VICTORIA STATION for DORKING. The Battalion was billeted in Dorking and the villages of NORTH HOLMWOOD, MID HOLMWOOD and SOUTH HOLMWOOD, under arrangements made two days previously by billeting parties consisting of 2 Officers and 30 other ranks.	
11th January 1915.	The new Double-Company system adopted in the Battalion for drill and training.	
13th January 1915.	Fortnightly Regimental courses of instruction for Officers and N.C.O.'s in Musketry, instituted.	
22nd January 1915.	The Battalion, as part of the 2nd London Reserve Division inspected by Lord Kitchener on Epsom Downs.	
24th January 1915.	Issue of rifles of Japanese pattern to the Battalion. Up to this date the Battalion has only had 180 rifles and musketry instruction has been carried on with difficulty.	
4.30 p.m. 26th January. DORKING.	Armed picquet furnished on the GUILDFORD - DORKING road with orders to stop and examine all vehicles between 4.30 p.m. and 8 a.m. on the following day. Strength of picquet - 1 Captain, 1 Subaltern, 2 Sergeants, 2 Corporals and 20 men.	
4.30 p.m. 27th January.	ditto.	ditto.
4.30 p.m. 28th January.	ditto.	ditto.
30th January 1915.	New organization of Companies finally adopted.	
	As regards the training, up to the 11th instant Company Commanders have been carrying out Company Training in the neighbourhood of BETCHWORTH	

(73989) W.4141—463. 400,000. 9/14. H.&J.Ltd. Forms/C. 2118/10.

Army Form C. 2118.

WAR DIARY
or
INTELLIGENCE SUMMARY.
(Erase heading not required.)

Instructions regarding War Diaries and Intelligence Summaries are contained in F.S. Regs., Part II and the Staff Manual respectively. Title pages will be prepared in manuscript.

Hour, Date, Place	Summary of Events and Information	Remarks and references to Appendices
30th January (contd.)	BETCHWORTH PARK.	
	Since the 11th instant particular attention has been given to the double Company drill.	
	Lectures have been given daily by Officers to Companies and platoons on the work of a Company.	
	(Sd.) R. G. HALES	
	Lieut. Colonel.	
	4.2.15	

"Battn. Copy"

2/15th Battn. London Regt.

Dorking

War Diary

1st to 28th Feby (inc) 1915

Army Form C. 2118.

WAR DIARY
or
INTELLIGENCE SUMMARY.
(Erase heading not required.)

Instructions regarding War Diaries and Intelligence Summaries are contained in F.S. Regs., Part II. and the Staff Manual respectively. Title pages will be prepared in manuscript.

Place	Date	Hour	Summary of Events and Information	Remarks and references to Appendices
Dorking	1/2/1915.		Recruits carried out miniature range Practice at Anstie Grange.	
"	5/2/1915.		48 men selected for the next draft to the 1st. Battalion carried out miniature Range Practice. Captain A.D.Bell rejoined the Battalion from the 1st. Battalion and was posted to the command of C. Company.	
"	6/2/1915.		The Second Class of Instruction in Musketry for Officers & N.C.O's finished.	
"	7/2/1915.		25 Recruits carried out Miniature Range Practice.	
"	8/2/1915.		The Battalion including outlying Companies attended Church Parade at the Parish Church of St.Martins	
"	9/2/1915.		The Battalion was exercised in taking up a defensive position under the direction of the Brigadier A.Field Party under Captain Turk proceeded to Reigate to take over the entrenching work from the 2/14th. Battalion.	
"	10/2/1915.		The guard at the entrenchments at Reigate wastaken over from the 2/14th. Battalion.	
"	11/2/1915.		The Battalion was engaged in entrenching at Reigate.	
		10.30 p.m.	A General Alarm was sounded. The Battalion paraded at the Battalion Alarm Post. The order to dismiss was received at 12.30 a.m.	
"	12/2/1915.		The Battalion was engaged on entrenching work at Reigate.	
"	13/2/1915		The entrenching work was not proceeded with owing to wet weather. Lt.A.W.Gaze proceeded to London to take charge of the Depot during the absence of the O/C.Depot on sick leave.	
"	14/2/1915.		Six Cooks commenced a course of instruction at the National Training School of Cookery Buckingham Palace Road. S.W.	
"	16/2/1915) 17/2/1915) 18/2/1915)		The entrenching work at Reigate was suspended on account of the unfavourable weather. "	
"	19/2/1915.		Lt.A.W.Gaze returned to duty from the Depot. The Battalion was engaged in entrenching work at Reigate.	
"	20/2/1915		The Battalion was engaged in entrenching work at Reigate orders were received for the Battalion to move to London on the 22nd. inst.	
"	21/2/1915.		Equipment was issued to every man in the Battalion.	
London	22/2/15. 11.55a.m. 12.40p.m.		The Battalion proceeed to London in two trains. 1st. train B.Co. & 2 platoons of C. Company. 2nd. train Remainder of Battalion. The men were dismissed on arriving at Somerset House & were billetted at their homes. Caretakers were left behind for the empty houses and three fellers for	

1577 Wt. W10791/1773 500,000 1/15 D.D. & L. A.D.S.S./Forms/C. 2118.

Army Form C. 2118.

WAR DIARY
or
INTELLIGENCE SUMMARY.

(Erase heading not required.)

Instructions regarding War Diaries and Intelligence Summaries are contained in F.S. Regs., Part II. and the Staff Manual respectively. Title pages will be prepared in manuscript.

Place	Date	Hour	Summary of Events and Information	Remarks and references to Appendices
	22/2/1915.		the guard on the Supply Depot & 2nd. Lt.C.J.Bowen was placed in charge at Dorking. Cpl.Thorogood and Pte.Randolp were gazetted 2nd. Lieuts. under date 21st. Feb. 1915.	
	24/2/1915		See 3 officers and 200 men were inoculated against typhoid fever.	
	27/2/1915.		A further number of men were inoculated. During its stay in London the Battalion carried out route marches with a view to recruiting and was exercised in Hyde Park and Regents Park.	
	28/2/1915.		The Battalion returned to Dorking.	
		9.40a.m.	lst.t.in A. and B. Company and 2 horses.	
		10.15a.m.	2nd train Remainder of Battalion.	

1577 Wt.W10791/1773 500,000 1/15 D.D. & L. A.D.S.S./Forms/C. 2118.

Army Form C. 2118.

WAR DIARY
or
INTELLIGENCE SUMMARY.
(Erase heading not required.)

2/15 London 1915

Instructions regarding War Diaries and Intelligence Summaries are contained in F.S. Regs., Part II. and the Staff Manual respectively. Title pages will be prepared in manuscript.

Place	Date	Hour	Summary of Events and Information	Remarks and references to Appendices
DORKING	Mar.1		*The Thrul* Musketry Class of Instruction for N.C.O.'s under Company Sgt.Major CLARK assembled for a fortnight's course.	
	" 3		A Draft of 42 men proceeded to the Imperial Service Battalion at WATFORD. 2nd Lieut. L.A. BALLANCE ceased duty on transfer to the 5th Battn. Kings Royal Rifle Corps.	
	" 4		One private joined the Imperial Service Battalion at WATFORD.	
	" 5		The Battalion took part with the 2/13th and 2/14th Battalions in an Outpost Exercise at HEADLEY HEATH.	
	" 6		A draft of 20 men proceeded to the Imperial Service Battalion at WATFORD. No. 1 Platoon fired a course on the Miniature Range.	
	" 7		Under instructions from the O.C. 2/4th London Infantry Brigade Sgt. GRAHAM and 8 men were sent to ST. ALBANS to take over vehicles and animals to be left behind by the I.S. Battalion. Capt. A. D. BELL and one corporal proceeded to WATFORD to take over the records etc. of the 1/15th Battalion. Lt. Col. HAYES T.D. having gone on sick leave MAJOR STRANGE assumed command of the Battalion (in accordance with Divisional Orders)	
	" 8		Lieut. PICKTHORN, one sergeant and 3 men proceeded to WATFORD to assist Capt. BELL.	

1577 Wt.W10791/1773 500,000 1/15 D.D.&L.   A.D.S.S./Forms/C. 2118.

Army Form C. 2118.

WAR DIARY
or
INTELLIGENCE SUMMARY.
(Erase heading not required.)

Instructions regarding War Diaries and Intelligence Summaries are contained in F. S. Regs., Part II. and the Staff Manual respectively. Title pages will be prepared in manuscript.

Place	Date	Hour	Summary of Events and Information	Remarks and references to Appendices
DORKING	Mar. 8		No. 2 Platoon fired a course on the Miniature Range.	
	" 9		Capt. OLIVER left for ABBOTS LANGLEY to take over the records of the 1/4th London Infantry Brigade.	
			Nos. 3 and 4 Platoons fired a course on the Miniature Range.	
			Capt. & Hon. Major MEALES with 10 N.C.O.'s and men proceeded to SANDWICH to arrange Billets for a Musketry Detachment.	
			Lieut. G.C. GRIMSDALE and 2nd Lieut. C.W.A. MILLER were transferred to the 1/15th Battalion.	
	" 10	11.34	4 Officers and 218 men under Lieut. A. W. GAZE proceeded to SANDWICH for Musketry.	
SANDWICH	" 11		5 Officers and 226 N.C.O.'s and men fired the new course for the Japanese Rifle.	
DORKING	" 12	1 pm.	The Musketry Detachment returned from SANDWICH.	
			The Battalion took part in a Brigade Exercise with 2/13th and 2/14th Battalions at HEADLEY HEATH.	
			Trooper B. E. PLATFIELD E. KENT YEOMANRY gazetted 2nd Lieut.	
	" 13		The 3rd N.C.O.'s Class of Instruction in Musketry was completed.	
			A Billeting Party proceeded to WATFORD to arrange for the billeting of the Battalion.	
	" 17		2nd Lieut. H. RUST joined for duty.	

1577 Wt. W10791/1773 500,000 1/15 D. D. & L. A.D.S.S./Forms/C. 2118.

Army Form C. 2118.

WAR DIARY
or
INTELLIGENCE SUMMARY.
(Erase heading not required.)

Instructions regarding War Diaries and Intelligence Summaries are contained in F. S. Regs., Part II. and the Staff Manual respectively. Title pages will be prepared in manuscript.

Place	Date	Hour	Summary of Events and Information	Remarks and references to Appendices
DORKING	Mar. 18		No. 5 Platoon fired a miniature range course.	
"	20		The B unoccupied house billets were inspected by the Officer Commanding the Brigade.	
"	22		No. 6 Platoon fired a course on the Miniature Range.	
"	23		The Battalion took part in a Brigade Exercise in the neighbourhood of LEIGH under the supervision of the Officer Commanding the 2/4th London Infantry Brigade.	
"			Remainder of Nos. 5 and 6 Platoons fired a course on the Miniature Range.	
"	24		No. 7 Platoon and the Machine Gun Section fired a course on the Miniature Range.	
"			2nd Lieut. P. W. LEWIS gazetted 17th March – joined for duty.	
"	25		No. 8 Platoon fired a course on the Miniature Range.	
"			2nd Lieut. A. W. HOUSEMAN gazetted 17th March joined for duty.	
"	26		Lt. Col. R. G. HAYES T.D. resumed command of the Battalion.	
"	27		The Order was received for the Battalion to move to WATFORD on Monday 29th April.	
"	28		Under Divisional Orders the Battalion Stores were loaded up.	
"			2nd Lieut. C. M. KILNER gazetted 18th March 1915 joined for duty.	
"	29		The Battalion left DORKING.	
		11.55	A & B Companies with 8 horses and 15 tons of baggage proceeded by the 1st train under command	

1577 Wt.W10791/1773 500,000 1/15 D. D. & L. A.D.S.S./Forms/C. 2118.

Army Form C. 2.

WAR DIARY
or
INTELLIGENCE SUMMARY.
(Erase heading not required.)

Instructions regarding War Diaries and Intelligence Summaries are contained in F. S. Regs., Part II. and the Staff Manual respectively. Title pages will be prepared in manuscript.

Place	Date	Hour	Summary of Events and Information	Remarks and references to Appendices
DORKING	Mar. 29		of Major STRANGE. COMMANDING OFFICER	
		12.53 p.m.	This party arrived at WATFORD.	
		Noon.	The remainder of the Battalion under the ~~and~~ with 8 horses and 15 tons of baggage left DORKING	
		1.53 p.m.	The Detachment arrived at WATFORD.	
WATFORD	" 30		The Battalion was engaged in training.	
			No. 10 Platoon fired a course on the Miniature Range.	
			The ~~Third~~ Fourth Course of Instruction in Musketry for Officers and N.C.O.'s was commenced.	
	" 31		No. 11 Platoon fired a course on the Miniature Range.	

Army Form C. 2118.

WAR DIARY
or
INTELLIGENCE SUMMARY.
(Erase heading not required.)

Instructions regarding War Diaries and Intelligence Summaries are contained in F. S. Regs., Part II. and the Staff Manual respectively. Title pages will be prepared in manuscript.

2/5 London

Place	Date	Hour	Summary of Events and Information	Remarks and references to Appendices
WATFORD	Apr. 1		No. 11 Platoon fired a course on the Miniature Range.	
	2		GOOD FRIDAY.	
	3			
	4		EASTER SUNDAY.	
	5		" MONDAY.	
	6		The Battalion took part in a Brigade Concentration march to LYEHOUSE. A Musketry Party of 5 officers and 210 other ranks proceeded to CHALK HILL Range to fire the new General Musketry Course authorised for Imperial Service Units.	Scheme App. I.
	7		No. 12 Platoon fired a course on the Miniature Range. The Musketry Course was not continued as the Range was unsafe (Divl. Order) 2nd Lieut. BERRY joined for duty.	
	8		No. 13 Platoon fired a course on the Miniature Range.	
	9		The Battalion was exercised in a Concentration March.	Scheme App. II.
	12		The Battalion took part in a Brigade Route march to HARTFIELD.	
	13		2nd Lieut. A. G. DOBRANTZ left to take up duty with the D.A.D.O.S., 2/2nd London Division. " " G. G. H. STONE reported for duty.	

1577 Wt. W10791/1773 500,000 1/15 D. D. & L. A.D.S.S./Forms/C. 2118.

Army Form C. 2118

WAR DIARY
or
INTELLIGENCE SUMMARY.
(Erase heading not required.)

Instructions regarding War Diaries and Intelligence Summaries are contained in F.S. Regs., Part II. and the Staff Manual respectively. Title pages will be prepared in manuscript.

Place	Date	Hour	Summary of Events and Information	Remarks and references to Appendices
WATFORD	1915 May 1		The Musketry Party continued the course at CHALK HILL RANGE.	
	3		The Battalion took part in a Brigade Rear Guard exercise in the neighbourhood of BOVINGDON and CHIPPERFIELD.	
			The Musketry Party continued the course.	
			2nd Lieut. E. F. ANDREWS joined for duty.	
	4		80 men began a course in physical drill and bayonet fighting under Lieut. RIMINGTON and 2nd Lieut. F. E. LEWIS.	
	5		Sgt. A.C.GIBSON rejoined from Course of Instruction ALDERSHOT GYMNASIUM.	
	6		Captain the Rev. A.C.B.WEST Chaplain to the 2/4th London Infantry Brigade was attached to this Battalion for billeting and subsistence.	
	7		The Battalion was warned to be ready to move at short notice.	
	9		The Battalion took part in a Brigade exercise in the neighbourhood of BOVINGDON and CHIPPERFIELD.	
			Pte. R.L.HOBSON gazetted 2nd Lieut. 6th May, 1915, joined for duty.	
	10		2nd Lieut. T.A.SMITH joined for duty.	
	11		2nd Lieut. L.R.RAY gazetted 11.5.15 joined for duty.	
	12		A Musketry Party of 160 men proceeded to CHALK HILL RANGE to fire the General Musketry Course.	

Army Form C. 2118

WAR DIARY
or
INTELLIGENCE SUMMARY.
(Erase heading not required.)

Instructions regarding War Diaries and Intelligence Summaries are contained in F.S. Regs., Part II. and the Staff Manual respectively. Title pages will be prepared in manuscript.

Place	Date	Hour	Summary of Events and Information	Remarks and references to Appendices
...FORD	1915 May 13		The Musketry Course was continued.	
			LIEUT. COLONEL R. G. HAYES T.D. left to take over the command of the 3rd Line Depot.	
			MAJOR E. F. STRANGE T.D. took over the command of the Battalion.	
	14		The Musketry Course was continued.	
			8 N.C.O.'s left for temporary duty at the 3rd Line Depot.	
	16		MAJOR E. F. STRANGE was gazetted Lieut. Colonel.	
			An advance billeting party under Lieut. RIMINGTON left for HATFIELD.	
...FFORD ...FFIELD	17	a.m. 8.30	The Battalion less Rear Party left WATFORD and proceeded by march route to HERTFORD where it was billeted with subsistence.	
...FFIELD ...TFORD	18	a.m. 9.30	The Battalion left HATFIELD and proceeded by march route to HERTFORD where it was billeted with subsistence.	
...NTFORD ...SHOP'S ...ORTFORD	19	a.m. 6.30	The Battalion left HERTFORD and proceeded by march route to BISHOP'S STORTFORD where it was billeted with subsistence.	
...SHOP'S ...ORTFORD ...FFRON ...LDEN	20	a.m. 6.30	The Battalion left BISHOP'S STORTFORD and proceeded by march route to SAFFRON WALDEN where it went under canvas.	
	22		Regtl. Q.M.S. HODGE gazetted Hon. Lieut. and Quartermaster of 3rd Line Depot.	

T2134. Wt. W708-776. 500000. 4/15. Sir J. C. & S.

Army Form C. 2118.

WAR DIARY
or
INTELLIGENCE SUMMARY.
(Erase heading not required.)

Instructions regarding War Diaries and Intelligence Summaries are contained in F. S. Regs., Part II. and the Staff Manual respectively. Title pages will be prepared in manuscript.

Place	Date	Hour	Summary of Events and Information	Remarks and references to Appendices
SAFFRON WALDEN.	1915 May 24		WHIT-MONDAY was observed as a Holiday.	
	27		One Warrant Officer and 7 men proceeded to LONDON for temporary duty with the 3rd Line Depot.	
	31		The Battalion took part in a Brigade Exercise in the neighbourhood of DEBDEN.	
			Lieuts. F.R.RADICE and A.C.H.BENKE joined for duty from the British Expeditionary Force.	
			Sgt. G.H.TRINDER rejoined the Battalion from duty as Range Warden at LONDON COLNEY.	

Lieut. Colonel.

2/15th Battalion - London Regiment.

Army Form C. 2118.

WAR DIARY
or
INTELLIGENCE SUMMARY.

(Erase heading not required.)

Instructions regarding War Diaries and Intelligence Summaries are contained in F. S. Regs., Part II. and the Staff Manual respectively. Title pages will be prepared in manuscript.

Place	Date	Hour	Summary of Events and Information	Remarks and references to Appendices

T2134. Wt. W708 –778. 500000. 4/15. Sir J. C. & S.

Army Form C. 2118.

WAR DIARY
or
INTELLIGENCE SUMMARY.
(Erase heading not required.)

Instructions regarding War Diaries and Intelligence Summaries are contained in F. S. Regs., Part II. and the Staff Manual respectively. Title pages will be prepared in manuscript.

Places	Date	Hour	Summary of Events and Information	Remarks and references to Appendices
SAFFRON WALDEN.	JUNE 1.		2nd Lieut. G.F.THOMPSON rejoined for duty.	
	2.			
	3.		2nd Lieut. R. MIDDLETON rejoined from Sick Leave.	
	4.		2nd Lieut. C.G.B.STEVENS - 1st Battn: joined for duty on leave from British Expeditionary Force.	
	5.	2.a.m. 2.30	Information received from BRIGADE MAJOR that Hostile Aircraft had been seen over Southend, Gravesend, Tilbury, Chatham. The Battalion was inspected by the Officer Commanding the Brigade.	
	7.		The Battalion took part in Brigade Night Marching exercise.	
	9.		2nd Lieut. F.T.MILEY joined for duty.	
	10.		51 C.S.M.CLARKE.G. 323 Co.Q.M.S.McINTYRE,J.S. 369 C.Q.M.S.HOOPER,N.D. 2963 Sgt.DRELKSON,E. 2858 Sgt.DURMENT,N.W. transferred to 3rd Line Depot.	
	11.		The General Musketry Course was resumed on the SAFFRON WALDEN RANGE.	
	12.		Lieut.C.J.BOWEN, & 2nd Lieuts.H.J.BACK, H.J.SPENCER, G.G.H.STONE, & T.A.SMITH transferred to 3rd Line Depot.	
	14.		The Battalion took part in a BRIGADE Outpost exercise at WICKEN BONHUNT. The General Officers Commanding the Third Army and the 2/2nd London Division were present.	
	15.		2nd Lieuts. HOUSEMAN & THOMPSON left to undergo a Course of Instruction at OXFORD.	
	16.		2nd Lieut. F.W.THOROGOOD returned from a Course of Instruction at PERIVALE CAMP.	
	17.		A Board of Enquiry was held on the loss of Official Bicycle No.84023.	
			50 Recruits under LIEUT. RIMINGTON were inspected in Physical Drill and Musketry by Lieut. General Sir A.E.CODRINGTON, K.C.B.	
	18.		The Battalion was inspected in Field Work at DEBDEN PARK by LIEUT.GENERAL SIR A.E.CODRINGTON,K.C.B. General Sir A.E.CODRINGTON was also present in the Final Assault Practice were also inspected.	

Army Form C. 2118.

WAR DIARY
or
INTELLIGENCE SUMMARY.
(Erase heading not required.)

Instructions regarding War Diaries and Intelligence Summaries are contained in F. S. Regs., Part II and the Staff Manual respectively. Title pages will be prepared in manuscript.

Place	Date	Hour	Summary of Events and Information	Remarks and references to Appendices
SAFFRON WALDEN.	JUNE (Contd) 18.		Notification was received that the Home Service men must be prepared to move on the 21st of June.	
	19.		London Gazette – Promotion – CAPT: W.T.KIRKBY to be MAJOR – LIEUT.T.L.ADAMSON to be CAPTAIN. 2nd LIEUT. R.MIDDLETON to be LIEUTENANT. All from 17th May.	
	21.		The Battalion took part in a BRIGADE OUTPOST EXERCISE at LITTLE CHESTERFORD.	
		12.30 p.m.	A Biplane with British Marks passed over going N.W.	
		4.30	The same Aeroplane passed over the Camp going S.W.	
			50 Recruits joined from the 3rd Line Depot.	
	25		The Battalion took part in a DIVISIONAL CONCENTRATION MARCH at BRENT PELHAM.	
	28		The Battalion took part in a BRIGADE OUTPOST EXERCISE at LITTLE WALDEN.	
			CAPTAIN W.F.A. NEWSON joined from 1st Battalion after recovery from Wound.	

2/15th Battalion – London Regiment.

1577 Wt. W10791/1773 500,000 1/15 D. D. & L. A.D.S.S./Forms/C. 2118.

WAR DIARY
or
INTELLIGENCE SUMMARY.
(Erase heading not required.)

Army Form C. 2118.

Place	Date	Hour	Summary of Events and Information	Remarks and references to Appendices
SAFFRON WALDEN.	1915 July 2		Musketry was discontinued temporarily on account of damage to the Range by Fire.	
	3		Two officers were called for as Reinforcements to 1st Battalion. Capt. W.F.K.NEWSON and 2nd Lieut. C.C.B.STEVENS detailed.	
	5		The Battalion took part in a Brigade Concentration Night March in the neighbourhood of WIMBISH.	
			Lieut. F. R. RADICE rejoined from sick leave.	
	7	a.m. 10.3	Emergency Alarm given.	
		p.m. 12.10	Order of dismissal given by Brigadier.	
	8		Home Service men inspected by Brigadier.	
			2/Lieut. F. J. SMITH 1st Battalion joined from sick leave from British Expeditionary Force.	
	9		Home Service men under command of CAPTAIN G. W. TURK left to join 105th Provisional Battalion in RICHMOND PARK.	
			Orders received for CAPT. NEWSON and 2nd Lieut. STEVENS to report at SOUTHAMPTON	
	10		Lieut. R. MIDDLETON transferred to 3rd Line Depot.	
			The Horse Lines were inspected by the Brigadier.	
			Capt. H.F.M.WARMN joined for duty from 3rd Line Depot after sick leave	
	11		Information received from Embarkation Commandant SOUTHAMPTON that CAPT. NEWSON and 2nd Lieut.	

Army Form C. 2118.

WAR DIARY
or
INTELLIGENCE SUMMARY.
(Erase heading not required.)

Instructions regarding War Diaries and Intelligence Summaries are contained in F. S. Regs., Part II. and the Staff Manual respectively. Title pages will be prepared in manuscript.

Place	Date	Hour	Summary of Events and Information	Remarks and references to Appendices
SAFFRON WALDEN.	1915 July			
	13		STEVENS embarked on the 10th.	
	15		Battalion Books inspected by the Brigadier.	
	26		2nd Lieuts. L. H. HART and F. E. GEARING joined for duty.	
	27		The Battalion took part in a Brigade Exercise in the neighbourhood of ASHDON.	
	29	10.0 a.m.	A Musketry party of 5 officers and 120 other ranks proceeded to MIMMS Rifle Range for Musketry.	
	30		Orders received to prepare numbers available over 500 as Draft for 1st Battalion. Draft selected and medically examined.	

Commanding 2/15th Battn. London Regiment.

Army Form C. 2118.

WAR DIARY
or
INTELLIGENCE SUMMARY.
(Erase heading not required.)

Instructions regarding War Diaries and Intelligence Summaries are contained in F. S. Regs., Part II. and the Staff Manual respectively. Title pages will be prepared in manuscript.

Place	Date	Hour	Summary of Events and Information	Remarks and references to Appendices
SAFFRON WALDEN.	1915 Aug. 2nd		Draft completely equipped.	
	3rd		Draft inspected by Brigadier.	
	6th		Hon. Lieut. & Quartermaster A. A. JOSLIN rejoined from sick leave.	
			A Medical Board was held on 2nd Lieut. F. J. SMITH, 1/15th Battn. (attached)	
	7th	p.m. 7.0	A Biplane (British) passed W. of camp flying N. W.	
	9th		Seven N.C.O.'s and men (Home Service) returned to the 105th Provisional Battn. for duty.	
			Lieut. K. W. M. PICKTHORN proceeded to join a course of instruction at CHELSEA.	
			2nd Lieut. A. V. JAMES proceeded to join a course of instruction at CAMBRIDGE.	
			2nd Lieut. A. D. WALLIS joined for duty.	
			Lieut. & Quartermaster A. A. JOSLIN proceeded on sick leave.	
	11th	a.m. 9.40	Biplane (British) passed W. of Camp going N. W.	
		p.m. 3.30	D.A.D.O.S. Division inspected hired tentage and ordnance stores.	
	12th		Inspection of Camp by G. O. C. DIVISION.	
	13th		Lieut. C. H. RIMINGTON attached to Brigade Bombing School as Assistant Instructor.	
	14th		Orders received for Draft to proceed to SOUTHAMPTON on 15th inst.	
			Capt. A. A. OLIVER rejoined from sick leave.	

1577 Wt.W10791/1773 500,000 1/15 D.D.&L. A.D.SS/Forms/C. 2118.

Army Form C. 2118.

WAR DIARY
or
INTELLIGENCE SUMMARY.

(Erase heading not required.)

Instructions regarding War Diaries and Intelligence Summaries are contained in F. S. Regs., Part II. and the Staff Manual respectively. Title pages will be prepared in manuscript.

Place	Date	Hour	Summary of Events and Information	Remarks and references to Appendices
SAFFRON WALDEN.	1915 Aug. 2nd		Draft completely equipped.	
	3rd		Draft inspected by Brigadier	
	6th		Hon. Lieut. & Quartermaster A. A. JOSLIN rejoined from sick leave.	
			A Medical Board was held on 2nd Lieut. F. J. SMITH, 1/15th Battn. (attached)	
	7th	p.m. 7.0	A Biplane (British) passed W. of camp flying N.E.	
	9th		Seven N.C.O.'s and men (Home Service) returned to the 105th Provisional Battn. for duty.	
			Lieut. K. W. M. PICKTHORN proceeded to join a course of instruction at CHELSEA.	
			2nd Lieut. A. V. JAMES proceeded to join a course of instruction at CAMBRIDGE.	
			2nd Lieut. A. D. WALLIS joined for duty.	
			Lieut. & Quartermaster A. A. JOSLIN proceeded on sick leave.	
	11th	a.m. 9.40	Biplane (British) passed W. of Camp going N.W.	
		p.m. 5.30	D.A.D.O.S. Division inspected hired tentage and ordnance stores.	
	12th		Inspection of Camp by G. O. C. DIVISION.	
	13th		Lieut. C. H. RIMINGTON attached to Brigade Bombing School as Assistant Instructor.	
	14th		Orders received for Draft to proceed to SOUTHAMPTON on 15th inst.	
			Capt. A. A. OLIVER rejoined from sick leave.	

1577 Wt.W10791/1773 500,000 1/15 D. D. & L. A.D.S.S./Forms/C. 2118.

Army Form C. 2118.

WAR DIARY
or
INTELLIGENCE SUMMARY.

(Erase heading not required.)

Instructions regarding War Diaries and Intelligence Summaries are contained in F. S. Regs., Part II. and the Staff Manual respectively. Title pages will be prepared in manuscript.

Place	Date	Hour	Summary of Events and Information	Remarks and references to Appendices
SAFFRON WALDEN	1915 Aug. 15th		33 N.C.O.'s/left as a Draft for the 1/15th Battn. British Expeditionary Force.	
			2nd Lieuts. W.S.H.SMITH, H.F.RUST, P.W.THOROGOOD and J.H.RANDOLPH promoted Lieutenant.	
	18th		Horse Lines removed to Audley End Park.	
			2nd Lieuts. L. H. HART and F. E. GEARING proceeded to a Course of Instruction at PERIVALE.	
			A draft of 39 recruits were received from the 3rd Line Depot and Administrative Centre.	
	19th	a.m. 7.12	A party of 5 Officers and 55 other ranks proceeded to NORTH MIMMS for Musketry.	
	20th		Lieut. & Hon. Major H. D. LEWIS promoted Captain. A draft of 4 recruits were received from the Administrative Centre. Capt. & Hon. Major H. D. LEWIS transferred to 3/15th Battalion London Regiment.	
	21st		The Officer Commanding Brigade inspected the Horse Lines.	
	22nd	a.m. 11.40	An aeroplane passed W. of camp and going N.	
			Lieut. & Quartermaster A. A. JOSLIN rejoined from sick leave.	
	25th		Draft of 14 recruits were received from the Administrative Centre.	
	27th 28th		Lieut. K. WILLS proceeded to WROTHAM for a course of Instruction in Pioneering. 2nd Lieuts. F.W.WESTMORE, J.A.C.FALKNER, and K.A.HIGGS joined for duty.	
			Col. LONG, War Office Staff inspected horses of Battalion in horse lines.	
	31st		2nd Lieut. F. W. LEWIS proceeded to a Course of Instruction at ALDERSHOT Headquarters Gymnasium.	

Confidential

War Diary of the

2/15th Battn. London Regt:

1 Sept: 1915   to   30 Sept: 1915

Volume 1.

Army Form C. 2118.

WAR DIARY
or
INTELLIGENCE SUMMARY.
(Erase heading not required.)

Instructions regarding War Diaries and Intelligence Summaries are contained in F. S. Regs., Part II. and the Staff Manual respectively. Title pages will be prepared in manuscript.

Place	Date	Hour	Summary of Events and Information	Remarks and references to Appendices
SAFFRON WALDEN	1915 Sept. 2nd		The Battalion Transport half-loaded was inspected by the Brigadier.	
	3rd		A Musketry Party of 50 left for MIMMS Range to carry out the modified General Musketry Course with the Japanese Rifle.	
	6th		A Detachment of 3 Officers and 150 men and the Battalion Transport took part in a Brigade Convoy Action.	
	8th	p.m. 9.40	Warnings were received that hostile airships had been seen over HUNSTANTON making for CAMBRIDGE and LONDON.	
		p.m. 11.40	The Guard reported the approach of a hostile airship coming from S.W. direction. The Battalion was turned out and scattered to the special alarm posts. The airship of the ZEPPELIN type crossed the parade ground and disappeared in a N.E. direction. At 1 a.m. the Battalion was dismissed	
	10th		The Battalion paraded as for an Alarm for the Composite Battalion composed of the 2/15th and 2/16th Battalions and was inspected by the Brigadier in AUDLEY END NORTH PARK.	
	13th		2nd Lieut. B. PEATFIELD left to attend a Course of Instruction in Musketry at BISLEY.	
	16th		The Battalion Transport was inspected by the O. C., A. S. C.	
	19th		2nd Lieut. F. T. BAILEY left for a course of Instruction in Transport Duties at PARK ROYAL.	

Army Form C. 2118.

WAR DIARY
or
INTELLIGENCE SUMMARY.

(Erase heading not required.)

Instructions regarding War Diaries and Intelligence Summaries are contained in F. S. Regs., Part II. and the Staff Manual respectively. Title pages will be prepared in manuscript.

Place	Date	Hour	Summary of Events and Information	Remarks and references to Appendices
SAFFRON WALDEN	1915 Sept 23rd		The Battalion took part in the concentration of the Mobile Brigade in QUENDON PARK and was inspected by the G. O. C. 60th (London) Division. A party of 9 other ranks under 2nd Lieut. E. E. ANDREWS left to attend a Machine Gun Course at BISHOP'S STORTFORD.	
	27th		The Battalion took part in a Brigade Outpost Exercise in the neighbourhood of HEYDON and bivouacked at GREAT ERESHALL.	
	28th		The Battalion returned to Camp.	

C.F. Stray Lt. Col.
c/o. 2/15th Battalion London Regiment,
(P.W.O.) Civil Service Rifles.

Army Form C. 2118.

WAR DIARY
or
INTELLIGENCE SUMMARY.
(Erase heading not required.)

Instructions regarding War Diaries and Intelligence Summaries are contained in F. S. Regs., Part II. and the Staff Manual respectively. Title pages will be prepared in manuscript.

Place	Date	Hour	Summary of Events and Information	Remarks and references to Appendices
	Oct.			
SAFFRON WALDEN	1 - 4		Nothing of special interest	
	5		Divisional Manoeuvres commenced	
		6.43 a.m.	Battalion in Brigade left SAFFRON WALDEN	
STEBBING		1 p.m.	Battn arrived at STEBBING and was billeted for the night	
	6	7.45 a.m.	Battalion left STEBBING	
BRAINTREE		10.15 a.m.	Battn in Brigade arrived at BRAINTREE and was engaged in a Divisional Tactical Exercise. After the exercise the Battn was billeted at BRAINTREE. One Draught horse died of colic.	
	7	7.45 a.m.	Battn in Brigade left BRAINTREE	
STEBBING		10.30 a.m.	Battn in Brigade arrived at STEBBING and was billeted.	
	8	7.45 a.m.	Battn in Brigade left STEBBING	
SAFFRON WALDEN		2 p.m.	Battn in Brigade arrived at SAFFRON WALDEN and was dismissed to Camp.	
	11		Orders received for Billeting Officer to proceed to BISHOPS STORTFORD.	
	13	9 p.m.	Information received from Brigade that a Zeppelin had passed over SAFFRON WALDEN proceeding in the direction of LONDON.	
	14		Battn took part in a Divisional exercise (trench fighting) near FURNEAUX PELHAM where the Battn was billeted for the night.	

Army Form C. 2118.

WAR DIARY
or
INTELLIGENCE SUMMARY.
(Erase heading not required.)

Instructions regarding War Diaries and Intelligence Summaries are contained in F. S. Regs., Part II. and the Staff Manual respectively. Title pages will be prepared in manuscript.

Place	Date	Hour	Summary of Events and Information	Remarks and references to Appendices
SAFFRON WALDEN	Oct. 16		Battn marched back to Camp at SAFFRON WALDEN	
	18		Battn informed that the 179th INFANTRY BRIGADE would move into billets at BISHOPS STORTFORD 26.10.15	
	17 & 18th		Nothing of interest.	
	19		Battn marched as advanced guard to the 179th INFANTRY BRIGADE to STEBBING where it took up a line of outposts covering the billets of the BRIGADE.	
	20		BRIGADE marched to WHITE NOTLEY where the Division occupied trenches and the 15th and 16th Battns were in divisional reserve. BRIGADE was billeted in BRAINTREE.	
	21		Division retired as a rear-guard: each brigade retired in echelon, 179th INF. BDE. on the right (north) flank. Battn was billeted at STEBBING GREEN.	
	22		Battn marched back in Brigade to camp at SAFFRON WALDEN.	
	23 & 24th		Nothing of interest	
	25		44 men transferred to 3/15th Battn Ldn. Regt., 4 men to 105th Provisional Battn.	
	26		Battn marched to BISHOPS STORTFORD where it took up its billets in the HOCKERILL area. Lt. RUST remained at SAFFRON WALDEN in charge of a rear party.	
BISHOPS STORTFORD	27		On arrival at BISHOPS STORTFORD the Battn took over duty as Battn in Brigade waiting.	
	28		Lt. RADICE appointed Instructor and Lt. C.H.RIMINGTON Asst. Instructor of Brigade Bombing School	

Army Form C. 2118.

WAR DIARY
or
INTELLIGENCE SUMMARY.
(Erase heading not required.)

Instructions regarding War Diaries and Intelligence Summaries are contained in F. S. Regs., Part II. and the Staff Manual respectively. Title pages will be prepared in manuscript.

Place	Date	Hour	Summary of Events and Information	Remarks and references to Appendices
BISHOPS STORTFORD	Oct. 29		A conference on the manoeuvres of 19-22/10/15 was held at the DRILL HALL, BISHOPS STORTFORD. Capt. A.G.T.HANES, M.O.I/c attached to 2/13th Battn. Capt I.D.STUBBS, M.O.I/c 2/14th Battn took over temporary medical charge of the Battn.	
	30 & 31st		Nothing of interest.	

Lieut. Colonel. Acting Adjutant.
2/15th Battalion London Regt.

Army Form C. 21

WAR DIARY
or
INTELLIGENCE SUMMARY.
(Erase heading not required.)

Instructions regarding War Diaries and Intelligence Summaries are contained in F. S. Regs., Part II. and the Staff Manual respectively. Title pages will be prepared in manuscript.

Place	Date	Hour	Summary of Events and Information	Remarks and references to Appendices
Bishop's Stortford	1.11.15	6.30a.m.	Lt.A.C.H.Benke began 7 days duty with the Q.M. for instruction in supply etc The Battalion ceased to be in Brigade waiting at reveille The Medical Board arranged for this day was postponed to 3.11.15	auq
	2.11.15		Officers attended a lecture by Major G.Hutchison, G.S. 3rd Army on "The Occupation of Trenches"	auq
	3.11.15	3p.m.	The Medical Board met at Headquarters (Battalion)	KNMP
	4.11.15	3 p.m.	The Battalion(with the 179th & 180th INFANTRY BRIGADES) took part in a tactical exercise: Court of Enquiry (Pres: Major F.J.Brett) at Battalion Headquarters. Subject-Damaged wall at STEBBING school-house	KNMP
	5.11.15		Nothing of interest	KNMP
	6.11.15	9.30a.m. 10 a.m.	"A" Company inspected in Physical Drill by the Assistant Inspector of Gymnasia C.F. CAPT.A.E.SAUNDERS was a member of D.C.M. at 179th INFANTRY BRIGADE	KNMP
	7.11.15		Nothing of interest	KNMP
	8.11.15		Nothing of interest	KNMP
	9.11.15		2nd Lt.F.J.SMITH detailed to attend a course assembling at PEMBROKE COLLEGE CAMBRIDGE 22.11.15 Lt.K.A.WILLS attached for a week to the Q.M. and 2nd Lt.R.L.HOBSON TO THE M.G.O. for a fortnight for instruction.	KNMP
	10.11.15		Court of Enquiry (President Major W.T.Kirkby) loss of Pole Bar of Wagon G.S.	KNMP
	11.11.15		Lt.W.S.H.SMITH appointed Brigade Machine Gun Officer Nothing of interest	KNMP
	12.11.15		2nd Lt.L.H.HART attached to Officer i/c Signal Section for instruction Received 525 .303 C.L.M.L.E. rifles	KNMP
	13.11.15		Nothing of interest	KNMP
	14/15.11.15		Sent away 521 Japanese rifles & 106430 rounds ammunition to Weedon Court of Enquiry (Majors F.J.Brett) damage to Battalion cart.	KNMP

Army Form C. 2118.

WAR DIARY
or
INTELLIGENCE SUMMARY.
(Erase heading not required.)

Instructions regarding War Diaries and Intelligence Summaries are contained in F. S. Regs., Part II. and the Staff Manual respectively. Title pages will be prepared in manuscript.

Place	Date	Hour	Summary of Events and Information	Remarks and references to Appendices
Bishop's Stortford	16.11.15		Lt.F.R.RADICE gazetted Captain	Kmmp
	17.11.15		4 men transferred to 105th Provisional Battn 2nd Lt. L.R.RAY attached for instruction to the Q/M. Lt.J.H.RANDOLPH & C.S.M. BASSETT detailed for a course at CHELSEA commencing 22.11.15 2nd Lt. R.L.HOBSON & 2nd Lt. L.R.RAY for a course at CAMBRIDGE commencing 22.11.15	Kmmp
	18.11.15		Nothing of interest	Kmmp
	19.11.15		Nothing of interest	Kmmp
	20.11.15		10 men transferred to 3/15th Battalion	Kmmp
	21.11.15		Billeting party sent to WARE	Kmmp
	22.11.15		Nothing of interest	Kmmp
	23.11.15		Court of Enquiry (Pres: Major W.T.KIRKBY) illegal absence of No.4413 Pte.A.J.Thomas 12 men appeared before a Medical Board	Kmmp
	24.11.15		Nothing of interest	Kmmp
	25.11.15		Services of CAPT.A.E.SAUNDERS placed at the disposal of the Division from 22.11.15 to 10.12.15	Kmmp auth
	26.11.15		Battn ordered to move to WARE on 29th inst; Lt.RUST detailed as O.C. Rear Party	Kmmp auth
	27.11.15		Nothing of interest	auth
	28.11.15			
W A R E	29.11.15		Battn moved to WARE by March route.	1/Col auth
	30.11.15		Detachment under Capt.F.F.TARVER & 2Lt.J.A.D.WALLIS consisting of 1Sgt 1Cpl,& 12 men proceeded to HERTFORD HEATH.	auth

E.F.Skrupp
Lt. Col.

CONFIDENTIAL

War Diary of

the 2/15th Battalion London Regiment

from 1st December 1915 to 31st December 1915

Volume 1

Army Form C. 2.

WAR DIARY
or
INTELLIGENCE SUMMARY.
(Erase heading not required.)

Instructions regarding War Diaries and Intelligence Summaries are contained in F. S. Regs., Part II. and the Staff Manual respectively. Title pages will be prepared in manuscript.

Place	Date	Hour	Summary of Events and Information	Remarks and references to Appendices
WARE	Dec 1		Company Training	aug.
"	2		Company Training: Billeting and feeding arrangements inspected by the A.A.&Q.M.G and the Sanitary Officer 60th (Kent) Division	aug.
"	3		Battalion Drill	aug.
"	4		Company Training Foot and Kit inspection	aug.
"	5	am 9.45	Church Parade	aug.
"	6		LIEUT. W.S.H. SMITH and 2 Corporals and 14 men of the Machine Gun Section left for BISHOPS STORTFORD to train under Brigade arrangements. Battalion Drill	aug.
"	7		Brigade concentration scheme MUCH HADAM. The G.O.C in C. Third Army was present. 2nd LIEUT HIGGS left for French fighting course at KELVEDON.	Appendix A aug.
"			LIEUT WILLS and 2nd LIEUT HOUSEMAN with 16 N.C.O.'s and men left to establish a detached post at STANSTED ABBOTS	authority 2/5.74/c
"	8		Company Training	aug.
"	9	10.30	The Battalion was inspected by COLONEL BAIRD commanding the 179th Infantry Brigade.	aug.

Army Form C. 2118.

WAR DIARY
or
INTELLIGENCE SUMMARY.
(Erase heading not required.)

Instructions regarding War Diaries and Intelligence Summaries are contained in F.S. Regs., Part II. and the Staff Manual respectively. Title pages will be prepared in manuscript.

Place	Date	Hour	Summary of Events and Information	Remarks and references to Appendices
WARE	Dec. 10		Company Training : Battalion night Concentration march.	appendix B awg.
"	11		Company Training. Kit inspections	awg.
"	12	9.45	Church Parade.	awg.
"	13		Battalion Drill. 2nd LIEUT. C.F. CLEGG joined for duty.	awg.
"	14		Battalion Concentration march.	awg.
"	15		Battalion Drill. Officers' Tactical Exercise	app. C. awg.
"	16		The detached post at HERTFORD HEATH was relieved by B Company. Convoy Scheme. Board for Stocktaking of Battalion Stores assembled.	awg.
"	17		Company Training.	awg.
"	18		Company Training. Kit inspections. 2nd LIEUT HIGGS reported from French Fighting Course.	awg.
"	19	9 am 9.45	Church Parade	
"	20		Company Training	awg
"	21		The Battalion was inspected by Brig MAJOR. GENERAL E.S. BULFIN C.V.O. C.B. commanding the 60th (Lond) Division 10 men were transferred to 3rd line to reduce strength to 600	authority T.F. RECORDS 15/30085/15 awg.

Army Form C. 2118.

WAR DIARY
or
INTELLIGENCE SUMMARY.
(Erase heading not required.)

Instructions regarding War Diaries and Intelligence Summaries are contained in F.S. Regs., Part II. and the Staff Manual respectively. Title pages will be prepared in manuscript.

Place	Date	Hour	Summary of Events and Information	Remarks and references to Appendices
WARE	Dec 21		The Detached Post at STANSTED ABBOTS was relieved by C Company.	aug
"	22		Battalion Drill	aug
"	23		Battalion Concentration March.	
"	24		CAPTAINS A.E. SAUNDERS, T.L. ADAMSON, 2nd LIEUTS. L.R. RAY, A.W. HOUSEMAN and C.F. CLEGG were transferred to the 3/15th Battn.	aug authority A/1517/16 60 a (home) Divn.
"	25	10 a.m.	Christmas Day. Church Parade. His Majesty the KING'S message read out to the Troops by the Commanding Officer.	aug
"	26	9.45	Church Parade	aug
"	27		Holiday	aug
"	28		The Detached Post at HERTFORD HEATH was relieved by D company. Battalion Route march. Two Telegrams from Brigade asking if 350 recruits could be received	aug
"	29		Battalion Drill. Officers Tactical Exercise.	aug Offr. D
"	30		Intimation received from O/c 3/15th Battn. that he is instructed to send draft of 350. 3rd of January fixed.	
"	31		Battalion Drill	aug

F. Offner
Major
for Lt. Col. clg 2/15th Battalion London Regiment,
(P.W.O.) Civil Service Rifles.

Appendix A.

Brigade Concentration March
6 December 1915.

2/15th Battn. London Regiment.

53, High Street, Ware.
6th December, 1915.

BRIGADE CONCENTRATION MARCH - TUESDAY
7th December, 1915.

Map reference Ord. Survey Sheet 29.
1 inch equals 2 miles.

The Battalion will concentrate at the road junction E. of point 182 on the BARWICK - HADHAM CROSS roads, facing E., at 11.14 a.m.

ROUTES.

"C" Company: STANDON ROAD - road junction E. of H in STANDON GREEN END - road junction N. of K in BARWICK - point 182. Leave "CANNONS" 9.4 a.m.

"B" Company: STANDON ROAD - road junction at point 254 - THORNRIDGE - road fork N. of F in SAWTREES FARM. Leave Town Hall at 9.15 a.m.

"A" Company: NEW ROAD - NEWHALL GREEN - cross road E. of NEWHALL - BAKERS END - road fork N. of F in SAWTREES FARM. Leave CHRIST CHURCH 9.19 a.m.

Local protection will be provided to point of concentration. Times of starting are those for the main body of each column.

Transport, fully loaded, will accompany "B" Company.
Headquarters, Signallers/Band, and Stretcher Bearers with "B" Company.
Machine Gun Section with their Companies

NOTES. Transport. Sufficient transport for dealing with supplies will be left behind.

The Company on Duty will furnish a loading party of 1 N.C.O. and 12 men to report at the Q.M. Stores at 8.15 a.m.

A Haversack ration will be carried.

Companies will parade as strong as possible and Marching Out States must be furnished to the Orderly Room by 8 a.m.

A. W. GAZE
Captain and Adjutant.

2/15th Battalion London Regiment.

Scheme for Officers 6th December, 1915.

DEFENCE OF A VILLAGE.

Reference: Ordnance Survey Sheet 29.   1" = 2 miles.

SPECIAL IDEA.

An Invading Force (Brown) after an advance on LONDON from the North has been checked and has retired North of the RIVER LEA where it is ordered to take up a defensive position and await reinforcements. The section, to which the 2/15th Battalion is detailed is from D of STAPLEFORD inclusive - TONWELL - cross roads at 2nd L of WADESMILL. Half-battalion (Officers only) of 2/15th Battalion at TONWELL which is to be put in a state of defence.

WORK REQUIRED.

Officers will rendezvous at TONWELL at 10.15 a.m.

Sketching materials, compasses, etc. to be brought; also F. S. Pocket Book, and Manuals of Engineering and of Map reading, etc.

Officers will be detailed in syndicates of 3.

Each syndicate will prepare

(1) A scheme of defence fully illustrated with plans and diagrams.

(2) Proposals for necessary supply depots working from cross road at W of WHEMPSTEAD.

(3) Billeting report, for 2 companies (war establishment)

(4) Schedule of demolitions required with detail of tools, explosives, etc.

E. F. STRANGE,

Lieut. Colonel,
Commanding.

Appendix B.

Battalion Concentration March
by Night.

B

53, High Street,
WARE.

10th December, 1915.

<u>2/15th Battalion, London Regiment.</u>

<u>NIGHT MARCH - 10. 12. 15.</u>

Ref. Ordnance Survey Sheet 29.
½ inch equals 1 mile.

The Battalion will practice a night march under strict service conditions this evening.

> Dress: Marching Order. Bayonets and ~~enetrn~~ entrenching tool handles are not to be carried.

<u>Point of concentration:</u> Cross roads N.E. of <u>N</u> in HODDESDO<u>N</u>.

<u>Time of arrival:</u> 6.25 p.m. - 6.30 p.m.

"A", "B" and "C" Companies will parade independently at Company Headquarters and march as follows :-

<u>No. 1 Column - "B" Company</u>: via LITTLE AMWELL - HERTFORD HEATH.

<u>No. 2 Column - "C" Company</u>: via GREAT AMWELL and road passing through <u>N</u> of STANSTED ST. MARGARETS On arrival at road fork S.W. of <u>G</u> in <u>G</u>.E.R., 2 platoons will be detached via road through <u>Y</u> of R<u>YE</u> HOUSE.

<u>No. 3 Column - "A" Company</u>: via STANSTED ABBOTTS - RYE HOUSE.

A cyclist will be detailed by O/C Signallers to accompany each column.

Machine Gun Section and Band will parade with their Companies.

Headquarters with No. 2 Column.

Each Column will take the usual precautions for safety in regard to motor traffic and will draw 2 lamps from the Q.M. Stores, one of which should, if possible, be a red lamp. These will be carried one at the head and the other at the rear of each column.

Advance and Rear Guards are not to be detailed.

A. W. GAZE

Captain and Adjutant.

Appendix B.C

Scheme for Officers' Tactical Exercise

Defence of a River

15 Dec 1915.

2/15th Battalion London Regiment.

TACTICAL EXERCISE.

15th December, 1915.

Reference: Ordnance Survey Sheet 29.   1" = 2 miles.

GENERAL IDEA.

1. A detached force strength approximately 2 Brigades is advancing from LONDON on CAMBRIDGE.

2. An enemy force strength unknown is reported to be in the neighbourhood of STEVENAGE.

SPECIAL IDEA.

You are Commanding Officer of a Battalion of Infantry and on arrival at Ware, you receive orders to hold the line of the river RIB from the crossing at WADESMILL to the crossing at Point 149 both inclusive.

Another Battalion is detailed to prolong to the left.

TASKS.

1. Select sections for companies and show dispositions on an enlargement 4" = 1 mile.

2. Make out a table of work for each Company.

3. Write a report on the above section of the river.

4. Write a report on probable enemy dispositions in case of attack on this position.

Officers are to arrange syndicates of 3 and rendezvous at point 254 at 10 a.m.; at WADESMILL at 12.30 p.m. for lunch and to meet the Commanding Officer.

E. F. STRANGE,

Lieut. Colonel,
Commanding.

Appendix D.

Officers Tactical Exercise

22 Dec 1915.

2/15th Battalion London Regiment.

RECONNAISSANCE OF A POSITION ON WHICH AN ATTACK IS CONTEMPLATED.

Reference: Ordnance Survey Sheet 29. 1" = 2 miles.

SPECIAL IDEA.

A composite Brigade of an Invading Force (White) moving East is ascertained to have taken up a defensive position on a general line Point 251 - Wood North-West of H in HUNSDON inclusive facing W.N.W. A Brown Force has arrived at WADESMILL and the G.O.C. decides to attack.

WORK REQUIRED.

Reconnaissance on the following points:-

1. Extent of the position.
2. Points of view.
3. Specially strong points likely to be of tactical value to the enemy - entrenchments, obstacles, etc.
4. Best line of attack.
5. Fire positions for attacker (including Field Artillery)
6. Flanks.

A panoramic sketch is to be prepared by each syndicate and enlargement of map to scale of 3" = 1 mile.

Officers are to work in syndicates of three. All work to be signed.

Officers will rendezvous at cross roads South of I in WARESIDE at 10.30 a.m.

Indications of position will be given by poletargets and signalling flags.

E. F. STRANGE,

Lieutenant-Colonel,
Commanding.

Duplicate

Confidential

War Diary
of
the 2/15th Battalion London Regiment
from 1 January 1916 to 31 January 1916
(Volume 2)

Army Form C. 2118.

WAR DIARY
or
INTELLIGENCE SUMMARY.
(Erase heading not required).

Instructions regarding War Diaries and Intelligence Summaries are contained in F.S. Regs., Part II. and the Staff Manual respectively. Title pages will be prepared in manuscript.

Hour, Date, Place	Summary of Events and Information	Remarks and references to Appendices
1916 Jan. 1 WARE	Company Training, Kit Inspection. Telegram received from 3/15th Battn that Draft would not arrive on 3rd inst.	an.9
2	Church Parade	an.9
3	Company Training. Officers' Revolver practice.	an.9
4	March with advanced guard to DATCHWORTH GREEN: thence with flank guards to WATTON.	an.9
9.45 a.m 5	Officers defending WESTMILL FARM. Battalion drilled by Acting Adj.	an.9 Appendix I
6	Defence of WESTMILL FARM. Arrival of C.S.M. PLACEY as physical drill instructor.	an.9
7	Route march with scheme SAWNSTED ABBOTS + ROYDON – HODDESDON – GREAT AMWELL – WARE.	Appendix II an.9
8	Foot and Kit Inspection.	an.9.
9	Church Parade.	an.9.
10	Company Training. Telegram received from London District that Draft of 253 Recruits will arrive from 3/15th Battn on 12th inst.	an.9.
11	Company Training. The outlying detachment from "D" Coy was relieved by "C" Coy.	an.9.
12	Information received from Brigade that London District had telegraphed that Draft would not arrive. Information received later from Brigade that Draft would arrive.	an.9
2:54 p.m	3 Officers and 130 Recruits arrived from 3/15th Battn.	
4.13 p.m	3 Officers and 119 Recruits arrived from 3/15th Battn. Captains SAUNDERS and ADAMSON, 2nd Lieuts HOUSEMAN, RAY, and CLEGG rejoined on retransfer from 3/15th Battn. The Battn was engaged in a lowry scheme. Appendix III	
13	Company Training. Lecture by Major CAMPBELL, Army Gymnastic Staff. 2nd Lt. CLEGG granted 5 days special leave. Medical examination of Recruits begun. Lt. Col E.F.STRANGE granted 3 days special leave.	an.9.
14	Company Training.	an.9.
15	Foot and Kit Inspection. Company Training.	an.9.
16	Church Parades. Lt. Col. E.F.STRANGE returned from leave. No 4957 Pte H.C.CLARIDGE demobilised for 2 months.	an.9. Authority C.R.,L.D. 19244
17	Company Training. The Machine Gun Section under Lt W.H.SMITH returned from Brigade Training at BISHOP'S STORTFORD.	an.9

Army Form C. 2118.

WAR DIARY
or
INTELLIGENCE SUMMARY.
(Erase heading not required.)

Instructions regarding War Diaries and Intelligence Summaries are contained in F.S. Regs., Part II and the Staff Manual respectively. Title pages will be prepared in manuscript.

Hour, Date, Place			Summary of Events and Information	Remarks and references to Appendices
	1916 Jan.			
11.30 a.m	18	WARE	Company Training. The Recruits and the Transport were inspected by Col E.W.BAIRD, Commanding the 179th Infantry Brigade.	awk
	19		2nd Lt. CLEGG'S leave extended to the 24th Jan.	awk
			The Battalion was engaged in a tactical scheme in co-operation with the Officers' School of Instruction at HERTFORD.	Appendix IV awk
	20		Company Training.	
8.36 a.m			An Advance Party consisting of Lt. H.F.RUST, Hon Lt & Q.M. A.A.JOSLIN, 2 Sgts and 18 Privates proceeded to WARMINSTER for LONGBRIDGE DEVERILL. 55 Recruits proceeded to BISHOP'S STORTFORD to appear before a Medical Board.	awk
	21		Clearing and loading preparatory to move.	awk
			Capt. A.E.SAUNDERS transferred to 3rd Line Depot.	
6.13 a.m	22		15 Officers, 413 Other ranks, 11 vehicles and 29 horses left WARE by train	Authority L.D.Orders 15. 8/1/16
8.15 a.m.			15 Officers, 377 " 11 " " 30 " " " "	awk
11.50 a.m		WARMINSTER	The First train arrived.	
2.30 p.m			The First detachment arrived at No 14 Camp, LONGBRIDGE DEVERILL.	
2 p.m			The Second train arrived at WARMINSTER.	
4.30 p.m	23	LONGBRIDGE DEVERILL	The Second detachment arrived in Camp. Sunday	
	24		Battn Route March. 2nd Lt. C.CLEGG reported for duty on expiration of leave	awk
	25		Company Training. 2nd Lt. C.CLEGG left on posting to the 3/15th Battn.	awk
	26		The Battalion in Brigade was inspected by General the RIGHT HON. SIR ARTHUR PAGET, G.C.B., etc Commanding the SOUTHERN COMMAND.	
	27		Medical Inspection of the Battalion.	awk
	28		Company Training.	awk
	29		Route March.	awk
			Foot and Kit Inspection. Physical Training etc. The G.O.C. 60th (Ldn) Division inspected the Camp.	awk
9.15 a.m	30		Church Parade.	awk
1.45 p.m	31		The 60th (Ldn) Division was inspected FIELD MARSHAL VISCOUNT FRENCH, G.C.B. etc COMMANDER IN CHIEF HOME FORCES. Strength of Battn on parade 30 Officers 712 Other ranks.	awk

D.J.Kauth Lt.Col
2/15th Battalion London Regiment,
(P.W.O.) Civil Service Rifles.

Appendix I.

Tactical Exercise for Officers.
5th/6th Jany. 1916

53, High Street,
WARE.

4th January, 1916.

2/15th Battalion, London Regt.

TACTICAL EXERCISE 5th/6th JANUARY 1916.

CLOSE DEFENCE OF A FARM.

REFERENCE: ORDNANCE SURVEY SHEET. 1" = 1 mile.

A Brown Force has taken up a defensive position on the Eastern bank of the river RIB from WEST MILL inclusive to K of KING'S inclusive. The 2/15th Battalion (representing 2 Companies at War Strength) is detailed to the defence of WESTMILL FARM. The enemy is reported at BULL'S GREEN.

Work required from Officers, by 9 a.m. 6.1.16 :-

1. Enlargement of map to scale 3" = 1 mile of whole position.

2. Ground plan and elevations showing proposed use of buildings, and supplemented by trenches, obstacles or other defensive works, water supply and communications.

3. Range cards.

4. General report on probable lines of attack and proposed means of defense.

E. F. STRANGE

Lieut. Colonel
Cdg. 2/15th Battn. London Regiment.

Appendix II

Report on work of Tactical Scheme.

7 January 1916

APPENDIX II.

                                                      53 High Street,
                                                        WARE, HERTS.

                                                        7th January 1916.

        <u>2/15th Battalion London Regt.</u>

           CONVOY SCHEME - 7th January 1916.

    The Commanding Officer wishes the following to be read to all ranks at a convenient opportunity:
    The work done by the men was, generally, very good, and the Commanding Officer noted with pleasure the keeness with which the somewhat arduous tasks were undertaken.
    The first attack by the BROWN Force was not well arranged, men advancing straight to their objective without deployment. On the other side the WHITE Force holding the position beyond ROYDON STATION abandoned it much too hastily and had to be sent back. With this exception and a similar want of tactical initiative on the part of the Officer Commanding BROWN Troops as they first entered ROYDON the tactical handling of the attacking force was in its main lines decidedly good, continued and successful efforts having been made to outflank the position taken up by the WHITE Force.
    In detail, however, the chief fault was lack of initiative on the part of N.C.O's in command of small parties who, when they came under fire, did not sufficiently quickly adapt themselves to circumstances.
    On both sides the flanks of detached parties chiefly under the command of N.C.O's were too much neglected and adequate precautions by use of ground scouts and advanced and rear points were not taken when moving on the road and the attention of Officers Commanding Coys is to be specially given to instructing their N.C.O's on these points which are of the very greatest importance for the security of men engaged in actual operations in the field.
    Officers Commanding Troops to which Transport of horses are detailed must make their own arrangements for feeding and watering at proper times, and in default of definite instructions on this point they must take the initiative in their own hands.

                                                              E.F.STRANGE.
                                                     Lieut. Colonel. Cdg.

Appendix III

Tactical Exercise 1.

12 Jany 1916.

Scheme and Special Idea.

CONFIDENTIAL

2/15th Battalion London Regiment

TACTICAL SCHEME 12TH JANUARY 1916

Reference. Ordnance Survey Sheet 29. 1" = 2 miles

Special Idea. Brown Force.

A Brown Army moving N.W. has established a Supply Depot at HITCHIN. On the 12th January a convoy of S.A.ammunition and tools proceeding by road to that place from WALTHAM ABBEY has arrived at the road junction S. of HODDESDON CHURCH at ten thirty a.m. with orders to proceed to HERTFORD. The O.C. then receives the following message:-

1.	2.	3.	4.
C E F S E	Q P O D N	F A U O N	I N S F C
P D O C E	F B A F Z	S A T P S	F C P V T
C B O C G	Z F D L R	B X M C S	H U E C S
L C R X G	C Y L E C	M C Z R V	I C K O K
S N M K B	F I Q S U	A V P S F	H A T O L
D I N S N	T N Z C G	O V K R N	Y P H F I

NOTE The convoy consists of 3 carts and 22 G.S.Limber Wagons and occupies on the road 310 yards. It will be represented by 1st Line Transport 2/15th Battalion extended to cover this space, and will proceed at a maximum average rate of 2 miles per hour from HODDESDON halting for 10 minutes at each ½ hour.

    O.C.Brown Force Capt. Warne

    O.C.Escort   Capt. Oliver

    Umpires Brown Force Lieut. Col. E.F.Strange
                    Major   F.J.Brett
                    Capt. & Adjt A.E.Gaze

1. Each Officer will send in an appreciation with decoded message attached of the position from the point of view of O.C.Brown Force at 10.30 a.m. 12.1.16 by 5 p.m. on 11.1.16 and O.C. Companies will also write operation orders as from the same place and time.
2. The Key word of the Special Idea is CYGNET (Playfair Cipher)

                                            E.F.Strange
                                            Lieut. Colonel

53 High Street,
WARE.

11th January 1916.

2/15th Battalion London Regt.

SPECIAL IDEA - WHITE FORCE.

TACTICAL SCHEME - 12. 1. 1916.

Reference: Ord. Survey Sheet 29. 1" - 2 miles.

You are the advanced guard of a raiding Force White acting against a Brown Line of Communications, WALTHAM ABBEY - HITCHIN. On the 12th instant, information reaches you at BAYFORD at 10.30 a.m. that a Brown Convoy is on its way to HERTFORD, which is securely held by immobile Brown Troops. You are ordered to attack and delay it until the arrival of your Main Body.

FORCE: Captain WARNE and "C" Company with 2 cyclists and bearer section.

PARADE: under your own arrangements.

E. F. STRANGE.
Lieut. Colonel.
Cdg 2/15th Battn London Regt.

Appendix IV

Tactical Exercise in conjunction with the London University O.T.C. School of Instruction.

19 January 1916.

Special Idea

2/15th Battalion London Regiment.

ROUTE MARCH & SCHEME.   WEDNESDAY 19th JANUARY 1916.

Map. Ref. Ord. Survey Sheet 97. 1" = 1 mile.

SPECIAL IDEA.

A Brown Force advancing Southward through HERTFORD consisting of one Brigade of Infantry has halted on the night of the 18th instant at STANDON. At 5 p.m. the Brigadier receives information that a Blue Raiding Force is collecting supplies in HERTFORD.

The O.C. Brown Force decides to continue his march on HERTFORD next morning, and details the 2/15th Battalion as Advanced Guard, which arrives at WADES MILL at 10.30 a.m.

NOTES.

The enemy will be represented by the Officers of the Hertford School of Instruction and by Red Flags each representing a Section of Infantry.

A. W. GAZE.
Captain & Adjutant.

Confidential

War Diary
of the
2/15th Battalion London Regiment

1 February 1916 to 29 February 1916

(Volume II)

WAR DIARY
or
INTELLIGENCE SUMMARY.
(Erase heading not required.)

Army Form C. 2118.

Instructions regarding War Diaries and Intelligence Summaries are contained in F.S. Regs., Part II and the Staff Manual respectively. Title pages will be prepared in manuscript.

Place	Hour, Date		Summary of Events and Information	Remarks and references to Appendices
LONGBRIDGE DEVERILL	Feb: 1st	4 p.m.	New Syllabus of Divisional training commenced; one N.C.O. & six men for BULFORD to draw 12 mules. Rear Party report returning by 3.56 p.m. on 2nd inst.	
	" 2nd		Route March. 12 mules taken on charge from BULFORD to complete establishment of L.D. Animals.	
		5.30 p.m.	Lieut. RIMINGTON with rear party reported on arrival from WARE.	
	" 3rd		Spring Drills. LIEUT.COL.E.F.STRANGE T.D. proceeded on leave. LIEUT. J.H.RANDOLPH returned from Grenadier Course GODSTONE. 2nd LIEUT.E.E. ANDREWS reported for duty on expiration of leave granted by 60th (London) Division on termination of duty at Divisional Machine Gun School.	
	" 4th		Spring Drills. Board of Enquiry assembled to enquire into the illegal absence of No. 3218 Pte. HARNOR G.F.	
	" 5th		Physical Training, squad drill, kit, foot and rifle inspections	
	" 6th		Church Parade.	
	" 7th	10.15 am	Second week of Divisional Training Syllabus commenced. 45 medically unfit appeared before Southern Command Travelling Medical Board. 2nd Lieut. S.G.BENNETT, ROYAL DUBLIN FUSILIERS joined for duty on attachment. CAPTAIN A.A.OLIVER and LIEUT.H.F.RUST proceeded on leave.	
	" 8th		Divisional Training Syllabus followed. LIEUT.COL.E.F.STRANGE returned from leave.	
	" 9th		Battalion Route March.	
	" 10th		Divisional Training Syllabus followed.	
	" 11th		Divisional Training Syllabus followed. A firing party was provided for the funeral of a Private of the Training Cen; R.A.M.C. T.Coy	
	" 12th		Kit and Foot inspections. CAPTAIN A.A.OLIVER and LIEUT.H.F.RUST REPORTED ON RETURN OF Leave CAPTAIN E.W.NEALES attended a District Court Martial WARMINSTER Major W.T.KIRKBY rejoined from duty at WARE as President No.7. Formation Committee.	
	" 13th		Church Parade	
	" 14th		Divisional Training Syllabus followed. Court of Enquiry re clothing etc found by the Salvage Party in billets in WARE after the departure of the Battalion.	

Army Form C. 2118.

WAR DIARY
or
INTELLIGENCE SUMMARY.
(Erase heading not required.)

Instructions regarding War Diaries and Intelligence Summaries are contained in F.S. Regs., Part II and the Staff Manual respectively. Title pages will be prepared in manuscript.

Place	Hour, Date	Summary of Events and Information	Remarks and references to Appendices
LONGBRIDGE DEVERILL	Feb: 15th	Divisional Training Syllabus followed. 2nd Lt.L.H.HART and No.874 Cpl E.C.G.WARD to attend Divisional Signalling Course	KLMP
"	16th	Intended Divisional exercise postponed and Divisional Training Syllabus followed. 16 men transferred to the 105th Provisional Battalion.	KLMP.
"	17th	Divisional exercise : see appendix. Report from Grenadier Course GODSTONE that LT.J.H.RANDOLPH qualified as a Brigade Instructor in bombing. CAPTAIN.T.L.ADAMSON detailed as a member of a Court of Adjustment held to the office of the A.D.M.S.	Appendix 1. KLMP
"	18th	Transport inspection at 9 a.m. Divisional Training Syllabus followed A.Coy on the Classification range.	KLMP
"	19th	Kit, Foot &c inspections. Squad drill & Physical training. CAPTAIN A.A. TARVER took over "A" Coy.	KLMP.
"	20th	Church Parade	KLMP
"	21st	Divisional programme followed. "A" Coy on open range. Horses inspected by INSPECTOR OF REMOUNTS, SOUTHERN COMMAND. Lt.K.A.WILLS & W.S.H.SMITH went on 4 days special leave & CAPTAIN A.W.GAZE on Sick leave.	and KLMP
"	22nd	Route march with protection.	KLMP
"	23rd	Divisional programme. B & C Coys on the open range. Number of men allowed to be away on Christmas leave increased to 10%.	KLMP
"	24th	Divisional Programme. Signallers inspected by Capt.FLADGATE. Lt.H.M. CARPENDALE (SOUTH WALES BORDERERS) left to rejoin his reserve unit.	KLMP.
"	25th 10 a.m.	Divisional Programme. C & D Rangex Coys on open range. Board of Enquiry at Brigade Headquarters re fire on 21/2/16 in Officers Qtrs	KLMP
"	26th	Kit and foot inspections.	KLMP
"	27th	Church Parades.	KLMP
"	28th	Divisional Programme. CAPTAIN GAZE *returned from sick leave*.	and Appendix 11.
"	29th	Battalion outpost Exercise. 4 men transferred to the 105th Prov: Battn.	

2/15th Battalion London Regiment,
(P.W.O.) Civil Service Rifles.

[signed] Lt Col

Confidential

War Diary

of

the 2/5th Battn. London Regt.

from 1 March 1916 to 31 March 1916

(Volume 2)

Army Form C. 2118.

WAR DIARY
or
INTELLIGENCE SUMMARY.
(Erase heading not required.)

Instructions regarding War Diaries and Intelligence Summaries are contained in F. S. Regs., Part II and the Staff Manual respectively. Title pages will be prepared in manuscript.

Hour, Date, Place	Summary of Events and Information	Remarks and references to Appendices
LONGBRIDGE DEVERILL		
1 March 1916.	Divisional Programme followed. 17 Recruits fired Parts IA and II A of General Musketry Course on open range.	aug.
2 "	Divisional Programme. Night Outpost Exercise. CAPTAIN H.F.M. WARNE proceeded on 10 days sick leave.	aug.
3 "	Divisional Programme. 150 mm trench digging. LIEUT. A.C.H. BENKE proceeded on 8 days special leave.	aug.
4 "	Kit and foot inspections etc.	aug.
5 "	Church Parades. 1 N.C.O and 6 men transferred to the 105th Provisional Battalion. 2nd LIEUT. B. PEATFIELD proceeded on 7 days sick leave. Church Parades. Battalion took over Divisional Duties	aug. aug.
6	Route march with scheme. 2nd LIEUT. A.V. JAMES and 2nd LIEUT. R.L. HOBSON proceeded on 4 days leave.	appendix I aug.

WARD DIARY
or
INTELLIGENCE SUMMARY.
(Erase heading not required.)

Army Form C. 2118.

Hour, Date, Place	Summary of Events and Information	Remarks and references to Appendices
LONG BRIDGE DEVERILL		
7 March 1916.	Divisional Programme followed. Firing & Mourning Party provided for funeral of 71 off men at Military Hospital & SUTTON VENEY.	nil.
8 "	Divisional Programme followed. Digging Party of 190 other ranks provided for Divisional Entrenchment. LIEUT. LEECH R.A.M.C. reported for duty as Medical Officer. 700 short C.L.L.E rifles drawn from Ordnance Depot WARMINSTER.	nil.
9 "	Divisional Programme followed.	nil.
10 "	Divisional Programme followed. Two men transferred from 71st Provisional Battn.	nil.
11 "	Kit, Foot & Rifle inspections. 60 Recruits posted into their Companies. 2nd LIEUTS HART and WESTMORE granted 10 and 6 days sick leave respectively.	nil.

WAR DIARY
or
INTELLIGENCE SUMMARY.
(Erase heading not required.)

Army Form C. 2118.

Instructions regarding War Diaries and Intelligence Summaries are contained in F.S. Regs., Part II. and the Staff Manual respectively. Title pages will be prepared in manuscript.

Hour, Date, Place	Summary of Events and Information	Remarks and references to Appendices
LONGBRIDGE DEVERILL 12 March 1916	Church Parade.	auth.
13 March "	Divisional Programme followed. Trained men and recruits firing parts 1A. 2A. G.M.C. on open range.	
6.30 p.m.	41 other ranks transferred from 105th Provisional Battn. arrived. CAPTAIN. T. L. ADAMSON. 2nd LIEUTS. HOUSEMAN, RAY, WALLIS and FALKNER transferred to 3rd Line Depot.	Authority London Dist Orders No 56(7) 6 March 1916 auth
14 March	Brigade Exercise, under direction of the G.O.C.	auth.
15 " 11. a.m.	Divisional Programme. The draft from the 105th Prov. Battn. was inspected by the G.O.C. at SUTTON VENEY CAPTAIN F.R. RADICE reported from sick leave.	auth.
16 "	Route march.	auth.
17 "	Divisional Programme followed. 2nd LIEUT. B. PEATFIELD reported from sick leave.	auth.

Army Form C. 2118.

WAR DIARY
or
INTELLIGENCE SUMMARY.
(Erase heading not required.)

Instructions regarding War Diaries and Intelligence Summaries are contained in F.S. Regs., Part II. and the Staff Manual respectively. Title pages will be prepared in manuscript.

Hour, Date, Place	Summary of Events and Information	Remarks and references to Appendices
LONGBRIDGE DEVERILL 18th Feb.	Kit, foot & rifle inspection. CAPTAIN H.F.M. WARNE returned from sick leave.	aufg
19 "	Church Parades.	aufg
20 "	Divisional Programme. CAPT. A.C. BAILY 1/5th ESSEX REGT. reported for duty on attachment. LIEUT. COL E.P. STRANGE proceeded to BULFORD on a senior officers course.	auf
21	Divisional Programme. CAPT. A. ATTFIELD 1/5th ESSEX REGT. reported for duty on attachment.	aufg
22 1.30 p.m.	Divisional Programme. Draft of 41 men received from the 105th Provisional Battn. inspected by the FIELD MARSHAL VISCOUNT FRENCH. 2nd LIEUT. H.J. SPENCER reported for duty from 3rd Tube Battn.	aufg
23.	Battalion in Tactical Exercise against 181st Brigade. MAJOR F.T. BRETT proceeded on 10 days leave. CAPT. A.A. OLIVER took over command.	aufg

WAR DIARY or INTELLIGENCE SUMMARY.

(Erase heading not required.)

Army Form C. 2118.

Instructions regarding War Diaries and Intelligence Summaries are contained in F.S. Regs., Part II. and the Staff Manual respectively. Title pages will be prepared in manuscript.

Hour, Date, Place	Summary of Events and Information	Remarks and references to Appendices
LONGBRIDGE DEVERILL 24 Mch.	Divisional Programme	a.w.y.
25.	Kit & Foot inspections. LIEUT. RIMINGTON. and 2ⁿᵈ LIEUT GEARING reported from leave.	a.w.y.
26	Church Parade	a.w.y.
27	Divisional Syllabus. 2ⁿᵈ LIEUT. F.J. SMITH proceeded on 4 days leave. LIEUT. WILLS on sick leave.	a.w.y.
28	Divisional Syllabus. Major W.T. KIRKBY left on transfer to the Territorial Force Reserve.	a.w.y. authority LONDON GAZETTE 25 Mch.1916
29	Divisional Syllabus.	a.w.y.
30	do	a.w.y.
31	Divisional Syllabus. Practice Gas Alarm by night. General musketry course commenced. Mobilization Ammunition 820,000 rounds MK VII drawn. LT. COL. E.F. STRANGE granted leave to 2ⁿᵈ April.	a.w.y.

Appendix I.

2/15th Battalion London Regiment

TACTICAL SCHEME FOR OFFICERS II.

Reference Ordnance Survey Sheet 122. 1" = 1 mile.

NARRATIVE

The BROWN Composite Brigade (179th) has remained in bivuac at LONGBRIDGE DEVERILL.   The 2/15th Battalion was relieved from Outposts on the 3rd inst.

At 10 p.m. on the 5th inst, the G.O.C. 179th Brigade receives reliable information that a WHITE force, strength about half a Brigade with attached troops, detached to strike at his communications with his main body is moving in the direction of WARMINSTER, under cover of LONGLEAT WOODS, and has arrived at WITHAM FRIARY.

He decides to march to HORNINGSHAM on 6th March at 10 a. m. and attack it.

1 Troop
Westminster
Dragoons.
1 Battery
2/5th R.F.A.
1 Section
2/4th Field
Company R.E.
2/15th Battn.
London Regt.
1 Platoon
Divl.Cyclist Co.
1 Section 2/4th
Field Ambulance.

An advanced guard as per margin is detailed to cover his advance.

All officers will write orders as O.C. Advance Guard to be sent to Orderly Room by 10 p.m. on 6th inst.

E.F. STRANGE
Lieut. Colonel.

> O.C.
> 2/15 Bn. London Regt
> P.W.O. Civil Service Rifles
> No. S.302
> -5 MAR.1916

SECRET.

REFERENCE: Ord: Sur: Sheet 122. 1" - 1 Mile

From O/C Advanced Guard
        179th Brigade
To.   O/C Cyclists attached

With reference to Operation Orders attached you will march at 8.45 a.m. tomorrow to HORNINGSHAM CHURCH where you will establish a communication post. Clear NEWBURY - SCOTLAND & POTTLE STREET of enemy troops, and patrol to LONGLEAT HOUSE and road fork West of H in HOOD HOUSE FARM.

Acknowledge receipt.

                                        A.B.GAZE
                                    Captain & Adjutant
George Inn
Longbridge Deverill
11 p.m.

Army Form C. 348.

MEMORANDUM.

From O.C. 1/4th L.F. Amb

To O.C. 1/5th Bn
London Regt

7/3/1916.

Attached please find
report of Casualties
in your unit during
operations 6th March 1916

Capt Ramet
for CO about on special duty.

RETURN OF CASUALTIES
OPERATIONS ON 6TH. MARCH

Slightly wounded and returned to Unit, N I L.

Wounded and taken into Ambulance.

Name	Initials	Rank	Reg.No.	Unit	Injury recd.	Time.
Bullock	H.	L/c	3063	2/15th,Bn.Lon.Rgt.) "C" Company	) Scalp wound	11.15 a.m
Nelson	V.	Pte.	3259	-do- -do-	Shot left) Scapula)	-.-
Stratton	H.C.	-.-	3453	-do- -do-	Shot right) Scapula)	-.-
Haines	A.S.	-.-	5102	-do- -do-	Scalp wounds	-.-
Bristow	J.W.	-.-	5085	-do- -do-	Wound in right) shoulder)	-.-
Jeffreys	W.J.	-.-	3524	-do- -do-	Scalp wounds	-.-
Wolfe	A.B.	-.-	5125	-do- -do-	Shot thro' jaw	-.-
Inskip	D.C.	-.-	3345	-do- -do-	Fractured patella	11-30am
Milem	H.	-.-	5107	-do- -do-	Shot in foot	12-15pm
Burgess	C.B.	-.-	3232	-do- -do-	Abdominal) wound)	-.-
Clifton	C.W.	-.-	5075	-do- -do-	Shot in leg	-.-
Janes	R.H.	-.-	5251	-do- -do-	Shot in knee	-.-
Roberts	D.H.	-.-	5205	-do- -do-	Shot in leg	-.-
Roper	W.A.	-.-	5157	-do- -do-	Scalp wound	-.-
Hammell	K.	Pte	5184	-do- -do-	Scalp wound	-.-

DIED

| Hill | F. | -.- | 3057 | -do- -do-) "D" Company) | | |
| Roberts | R.P. | -.- | 5113 | -do- -do- | | |

2/4TH LONDON FIELD AMBULANCE,
60TH (LONDON) DIVISION.

Capt R and
2/4 Lndn F. Amb.

Confidential

WAR. DIARY.

of

the 2/15th Battalion London Regiment.

from 1 April 1916 to 30 April 1916.

(Volume 2)

Army Form C. 2118.

WAR DIARY
or
INTELLIGENCE SUMMARY.
(Erase heading not required.)

Instructions regarding War Diaries and Intelligence Summaries are contained in F.S. Regs., Part II. and the Staff Manual respectively. Title pages will be prepared in manuscript.

Place	Date	Hour	Summary of Events and Information	Remarks and references to Appendices
LONGBRIDGE DEVERIL	April 1		General musketry course continued. Kit and foot-inspection. CAPT. C.H. ATTFIELD granted. 7 days leave.	auf.
"	2	7.30 a.m.	Church Parades.	auf.
"	3		General musketry course continued. LT. COL. STRANGE proceeded on a visit to the army in FRANCE. 100 men digging.	auf.
"	4		General musketry course continued. Lewis Gun team commenced firing Part II.	auf.
"	5		General musketry course continued. Lewis Gun team completed.	auf.
"	6		General musketry course not completed by 345 other ranks. CAPTAIN A.A. OLIVER gazetted major.	auf.
"	7	8.35 am 9.25	Practice alarm assembly. Battn reported ready to move. Brigade Route march and field exercise. 2nd Lt. K.J.B. Hunt returned from sick leave.	auf.
"	8		Kit and Rifle Inspection & Lieut. N.S.H. Smith left to attend a Lewis Gun Course at HAYLING ISLAND. LIEUT. K.W.M. PICKTHORN gazetted Captain to date 1 March 1916	auf

(73989) W4141—463. 400,000. 9/14. H.&J.Ltd. Forms/C. 2118/10.

Army Form C. 2118.

WAR DIARY
or
INTELLIGENCE SUMMARY.
(Erase heading not required.)

Instructions regarding War Diaries and Intelligence Summaries are contained in F.S. Regs., Part II and the Staff Manual respectively. Title pages will be prepared in manuscript.

Hour, Date, Place	Summary of Events and Information	Remarks and references to Appendices
LONGBRIDGE DEVERILL Sept 9.	Church Parade. MAJOR A.A. OLIVER proceeded on a visit to the Army in FRANCE, LIEUT. COL. E.F. STRANGE returned from a similar visit and resumed command.	auif.
" 10	General Musketry Course commenced by 112 all ranks from each of C and D Companies.	auif.
" 11	LIEUT. A.C.H BENKE gazetted captain to date 29 March FEB. 2nd LIEUT. R.L. HOBSON left to take up duty on admiralty intelligence staff. General Musketry Course continued. Remainder of Battn. digging.	auif.
12	General musketry Course continued. Ballalein Road march 2 officers 1 Sgt. 4 Cpls and 16 other ranks left for PERHAM DOWN for French mortar Course. F. M. C. continued.	auif.
13		auif.
14	G. M. C. continued. Captain E.W. NEALES transferred to 3rd Line. 2nd LT. K.A. HIGGS proceeded on sick leave.	Authority London Dist Order No 86 Nov. 5. auif.
15	Kit and Foot Inspections etc.	auif.

Army Form C. 2118.

WAR DIARY
or
INTELLIGENCE SUMMARY.
(Erase heading not required.)

Instructions regarding War Diaries and Intelligence Summaries are contained in F. S. Regs., Part II. and the Staff Manual respectively. Title pages will be prepared in manuscript.

Hour, Date, Place		Summary of Events and Information	Remarks and references to Appendices
LONGBRIDGE DEVERILL	April 16	Church Parade. MAJOR A.A. OLIVER reported on return from a visit to the ARMY in FRANCE.	amp
	17	General Musketry course continued.	amp.
	8.pm	General Alarm practiced, followed by Brigade route march. Strength on parade 784 all ranks.	
	18	General musketry course postponed on account of weather conditions. Other details digging etc.	amp.
	19	2nd Party completed. General musketry course.	amp
	20	3rd Party commenced General musketry course. Battn. Route march. Eleven officers attended lecture by G.O.C.	amp
	21	Good Friday. Church Parade. Lieut K.A. WILLS gazetted Captain	amp.
	22	That instructions etc. G.M.C.	amp.
	23	Easter Sunday.	amp.

(7,3959) W.4141—463. 400,000. 9/14. H.&J.Ltd. Forms/C. 2118/10.

Army Form C. 2118.

WAR DIARY
or
INTELLIGENCE SUMMARY.
(Erase heading not required.)

Instructions regarding War Diaries and Intelligence Summaries are contained in F. S. Regs., Part II. and the Staff Manual respectively. Title pages will be prepared in manuscript.

Hour, Date, Place	Summary of Events and Information	Remarks and references to Appendices
LONGBRIDGE DEVERILL April 24	General Musketry Course.	initl.
" 25	General Musketry Course.	initl.
" 26	do do de. Battalion Route March.	
" 27	General Musketry Course.	

Army Form C. 2118.

WAR DIARY
or
INTELLIGENCE SUMMARY.
(Erase heading not required.)

Instructions regarding War Diaries and Intelligence Summaries are contained in F.S. Regs., Part II. and the Staff Manual respectively. Title pages will be prepared in manuscript.

Hour, Date, Place	Summary of Events and Information	Remarks and references to Appendices

(73989) W4141—463. 400,000. 9/14. H.&J.Ltd. Forms/C. 2118/10.

Army Form C. 2118

WAR DIARY
or
INTELLIGENCE SUMMARY
(Erase heading not required.)

Instructions regarding War Diaries and Intelligence Summaries are contained in F.S. Regs., Part II. and the Staff Manual respectively. Title Pages will be prepared in manuscript.

Place	Date	Hour	Summary of Events and Information	Remarks and references to Appendices
LONGBRIDGE DEVERILL	April 28	1 p.m. 7.30	Alarm order received	cuff.
		9.30	Orders received that Battn. would proceed to IRELAND	
	29 -	1.30 a.m.	Entraining orders received.	cuff.
		2	One Officer and 25 other ranks left for WARMINSTER	
		3.55	17 Officers. 340 other ranks. 43 wagons horses and 12 wagons left camp.	
		6.20	This party left WARMINSTER STATION taking first party who were left out of previous train.	cuff.
		5	3rd Party. 10 Officers 314 other ranks: 3 wagons left camp.	
		8	10 Officers. 314 other ranks 3 wagons and 15 horses. Left. WARMINSTER STATION.	
		9.30 p.m.	2 Officers and 50 other ranks left. WARMINSTER STATION.	
NEYLAND	30	4.40	Battalion arrived at NEYLAND and camped. Marching in state 29 Officers 699 other ranks. 15 wagons. 3 carts 58 horses 10 bicycles. 10 A.S.C. Drivers.	
		9 a.m. 1 -	Church Parade. 8 Officers 300 other ranks to hold themselves ready to embark.	cuff.

Confidential

WAR DIARY
of
The 2/15th Battalion London Regt.

From 1 May to 31 May 1916

(Volume 2)

WAR DIARY or INTELLIGENCE SUMMARY

Army Form C.2118

Instructions regarding War Diaries and Intelligence Summaries are contained in F.S. Regs., Part II. and the Staff Manual respectively. Title Pages will be prepared in manuscript.

(Erase heading not required.)

Place	Date	Hour	Summary of Events and Information	Remarks and references to Appendices
NEYLAND	May 1	8.15 am	Orders received for 8 Officers and 300 other ranks to entrain at 11 am	
		9.30	Pte. R.M.W. SALE. A boy found to be suffering from measles, sent into hospital at PEMBROKE DOCK.	aug
		11 am	8 O. & 7 Officers and 300 other ranks entrained on S.S. RATHMORE	
		4 pm	11 Officers & 259 other ranks embarked on S.S. ARCHANGEL	
		9 ...	Both boats left. Pte. MILFORD HAVEN under escort of HMS MORNING STAR	
QUEENSTOWN	2	4.30 am	Both arrived at QUEENSTOWN. Voyage without incident.	aug
NEYLAND FOTAY.	3	8	Both detachments disembarked and proceeded to FOTAY PARK and camped. Balance of Battn. with Transport entrained.	
		10 pm	At FOTAY PARK.	
		5.30	Balance of Battalion with Transport arrived	
		8	Transport arrived. Two A.S.C. horses reported left behind at NEYLAND.	aug.
	4		In camp at FOTAY PARK	aug
	5		In camp at FOTAY PARK.	
	6	8 am	The Battn. moved out of camp en route for BALLINCOLLIG. Lieut. Root RUST and 12 O.R. left to fetch remounts from CORK and attached to 2/u U Battn.	
		8.30	72 Tents taken on steam lorry. Adjutant drew £300 in CORK from PROVINCIAL BANK OF IRELAND for advances to men.	
BALLINCOLLIG		4.30 pm	Brigade arrived at BALLINCOLLIG and were quartered in BARRACKS.	aug

Army Form C. 2118

WAR DIARY
or
INTELLIGENCE SUMMARY

(Erase heading not required.)

Instructions regarding War Diaries and Intelligence Summaries are contained in F.S. Regs., Part II. and the Staff Manual respectively. Title Pages will be prepared in manuscript.

Place	Date	Hour	Summary of Events and Information	Remarks and references to Appendices
BALLINCOLLIG	May 7	am	Brigade left BALLINCOLLIG and proceeded by march route to B. COACHFORD and encamped. Pte. HYDE A Coy admitted to hospital with measles.	auth.
COACHFORD	8	p.m. 1	Brigade left COACHFORD and proceeded to MACROOM.	
MACROOM		1 p.m.	arrived at MACROOM and pitched camp in park of MACROOM CASTLE.	
		11 a.m.	3 Officers and 100 men A Coy proceeded to BALLYVOGUE 7 miles to make arrests. No prisoners obtained.	
	9	2.15 a.m.	3 Officers and 100 men C Coy visited NUTLEY for the same purpose but made no arrests.	auth
"		3 a.m.	3 Officers and 100 men of B Coy visited several houses in MACROOM and made one arrest.	auth
		7 p.m.	Lt Col STRANGE proceeded to CORK to enter hospital. MAJOR A.R. OLIVER took over command.	
		11 p.m.	CAPTAIN WARNE and 3 officers and 100 men of D Company visited and made two arrests.	
	10.		At MACROOM orders received to move next day.	auth
	11		Column proceeded by march route to MILL STREET, and entrained	auth
MILL STREET.		p.m. 10.30	there, & left for ROSSLARE.	
ROSSLARE	12	am 5	Balln. arrived at ROSSLARE and embarked on S.S. CONNAUGHT. Transport on S.S. ZIPTAH.	auth
		p.m. 7	left ROSSLARE.	

1375 Wt. W.593/826 1,000,000 4/15 J.B.C. & A. A.D.S.S./Forms/C. 2118.

Army Form C. 2118.

WAR DIARY
or
INTELLIGENCE SUMMARY.
(Erase heading not required.)

Instructions regarding War Diaries and Intelligence Summaries are contained in F.S. Regs., Part II. and the Staff Manual respectively. Title pages will be prepared in manuscript.

Place	Date	Hour	Summary of Events and Information	Remarks and references to Appendices
ROSSLARE	May 12	pm		
FISHGUARD	12	10.30 pm	S.S. CONNAUGHT arrived.	
		midnight 12.	S.S. ZIPTAH arrived.	
		pm 11.	First Train left.	
		12. am	Second Train left.	
WARMINSTER	13	6.30	First Train arrived WARMINSTER	awy
		7.30	Second " " "	
			Transport arrived. Owing to action of R.T.O at FISHGUARD. Transport arrived in disorder and great difficulty was experienced in sorting out animals & vehicles. COL C de POTRON. LANCASHIRE FUSILIERS took over command	awy
	14		Church Parades.	awy
LONGBRIDGE DEVERILL	15		Company Training	awy
	16		Do	awy
	17		Do	awy
	18		Do	awy

2/15 Batt. London Regt.

WAR DIARY

or

INTELLIGENCE SUMMARY.

(Erase heading not required.)

Army Form C. 2118.

Hour, Date, Place			Summary of Events and Information	Remarks and references to Appendices
LONG-BRIDGE DEVERILL	May 19	a.m. 9	Ceremonial practice. Physical Training, Musketry, Bayonet Fighting and Cleaning Lines. Bombers course continued.	F.R.R.
		p.m. 8.30	The Battalion occupied the Trenches at Sutton Va SUTTON VENY by night. An attack was made on the position by an enemy represented by the Scouts and the supports were rushed up	
	20	a.m. 11.30	Kit and foot inspection. Bombers' course concluded Inspection of the camp by the C.O.	F.R.R.
	21	a.m. 9	Church Parades.	F.R.R.
	22	a.m. 7	S.M.C. continued; Casuals.	
		9	Coy Training	
		11.15	Ceremonial	
		8.30	The Battalion paraded for a Trench relieving exercise. The 2/16 Batt relieved the 2/16th Batt at 11.30; the relief being completed at 12.25 a.m. An attack was made on the left of the line by a raiding party of bombers during the night. Some repair of trenches and erecting of barbed wire were performed.	F.R.R.
	23	p.m. 1.30	2Lt L.H.O.HART proceeded on 21 days leave. Parade for ceremonial, musketry, bayonet fighting.	F.R.R.
	24	a.m. 7.5	The Battalion took part in the Divisional Route March 7.5a.m. to — NEWBURY — LONG-BRIDGE DEVERILL — BUCKLEY'S WOOD —	F.R.R.
		p.m. 2.30	Ceremonial, musketry, bayonet fighting.	

Army Form C. 2118.

WAR DIARY
—of the—
INTELLIGENCE SUMMARY.
(2/15 Battⁿ London Reg
(Erase heading not required.)

Instructions regarding War Diaries and Intelligence Summaries are contained in F.S. Regs., Part II. and the Staff Manual respectively. Title pages will be prepared in manuscript.

Hour, Date, Place			Summary of Events and Information	Remarks and references to Appendices
LONGBRIDGE DEVERILL	May 25	a.m. 10	G.M.C continued Company Training. Ceremonial. Outpost. Attack	F.R.R.
	26	a.m. 6:40	The Battalion took part in a Divisional tactical exercise. The 179th Inf. Bde. marched via LONGBRIDGE DEVERILL - PERTWOOD DOWN to KNOYLE DOWN FARM, where it concentrated. For the operations see index Appendix №5. The Battalion	Appendix F.R.R.
	27	a.m. 9	reached camp at 5.40 p.m. Lt F.T. BAILEY returned from leave Kit and foot inspection etc. Inspection by the C.O. of rifles and bayonets. 2Lt A.V. JAMES returned from leave.	F.R.R.
	28	a.m. 9:45	Church parades. 2Lt L.H. HART returned from leave	F.R.R.
	29	p.m. 1:30	Field Firing for A and B Coys Capt R.W. PETHORNE Mortlock C and D Coys see Appendix relinquishes	Appendix
	30	6:15	for duties H.M. the KING at HEYTESBURY	F.R.R.
	31	p.m. 8:15	Draft of 130 men arrives from 3rd Line Parade for Inspection of the 60th DIVISION by H.M. THE KING Capt R.A. WILLS ceases to be attached to Brigade Headquarters.	F.R.R.
	JUNE 1	p.m. 7.0	Field Firing for C and D Coys. 3 days Bombing Course for 8 men per Coy began. 10 party for embarkation leave goes off. including Capt A.C.H.BENKE, Lts H.F.TRUST, R.F.THOROGOOD, W.H.SMITH, C.PEAT, also 2Lt L.H. HART, B. SPENCER, C. KILMER.	

(73989) W4141—463. 400,000. 9/14. H.&S. Ltd. Forms/C. 2118/10

Confidential

WAR DIARY

of

the 2/15th Battalion London Regt.

from 1 June to 27 June 1916

(Volume 2)

2/15 Bn London Reg¹

WAR DIARY
INTELLIGENCE SUMMARY.
(Erase heading not required.)

Army Form C. 2118.

Instructions regarding War Diaries and Intelligence Summaries are contained in F.S. Regs., Part II and the Staff Manual respectively. Title pages will be prepared in manuscript.

Hour, Date, Place		Summary of Events and Information	Remarks and references to Appendices
LONGBRIDGE DEVERILL	June 1 2.0 p.m.	Field firing for C and D Coys. 3 Days Bombing Courses for 8 men per Coy begin. 1st party for embarcation leave goes off including Capt A.C.H.BENKE, Lts H.F.RUST, P.W.THOROGOOD, W.H.SMITH, B.PEATFIELD, 2nd Lt L.H.HART C.M.KILNER, J.H.SPENCER.	F.R.R.
	2	Coy Training	F.R.R.
	3	Coy Training. Inspection of the Draft by the C.O. On leave Maj. A.A.OLIVER, Capt A.W.GAZE. Lt C.RIMINGTON, J.H.RANDOLPH, 2nd Lt F.T.BAILY, S.S.THOMPSON, A.V.JAMES. go on leave	F.R.R. F.R.R.
	4. 6.50 a.m.	Church parade. Lt B.PEATFIELD returns from leave	F.R.R.
	5. 9.-	Coy Training. Draft and D Coy occupy the trenches at SUTTON VENY Second party for embarcation leave goes off. Capt A.C.H.BENKE, Lts H.F.RUST, P.W.THOROGOOD, W.H.SMITH B.PEATFIELD 2Lt L.H.HART, C.M.KILNER, J.H.SPENCER returns from leave. Capt F.E.TANNER Capt C.A.BAILY, 2nd Lt F.J.SMITH, F.W.LEWIS go on leave	F.R.R.
	6	Coy Training. G.M.E for Draft and Canals	F.R.R.
	7.	G.M.E continued.	F.R.R.
	8.	G.M.E continued. Capts F.R.RADICE, Lt W.A.HIGGS, F.E.GEARING, G.BENNET F.E.ANDREWS go on leave K.W.PICKTHORN	
	9.	Capt A.W.GAZE Coy Training. Maj. A.A.OLIVER. Capt A.W.GAZE. Lt C.RIMINGTON J.H.RANDOLPH, 2Lt F.T.BAILY, S.S.THOMPSON, A.V.JAMES. 2Lt S.S.BENNET goes on leave. 3rd party for embarcation leave goes off. 2nd party returns.	F.R.R.
	10. A.M. 10.--	Inspection of Battalion by the C.O.	F.R.R.

2/15 Bn London Regt
WAR DIARY
of
INTELLIGENCE SUMMARY.
(Erase heading not required.)

Army Form C. 2118.

Hour, Date, Place		Summary of Events and Information	Remarks and references to Appendices
LONGBRIDGE DEVERILL	JUNE 11 a.m. 8.50	Church Parades. Capts F.F.TARVER, C.A.BAILY, Lts F.J.SMITH, F.W.LEWIS return from leave	F.R.R.
	12	Coy Training. Digging party of 100 to SUTTON VENY. 3rd party returns from embarkation leave including Capts F.R. RADICE, K.W. PICKTHORN, Lts K.A. HIGGS, F.E. GEARING, G.S. BENNET	F.R.R.
	13 a.m. 9-	Battalion Route march LONGBRIDGE DEVERILL - WARMINSTER - LONGLEAT PARK - LONGBRIDGE DEVERILL. A Coy inspected by CO.	F.R.R.
	14	Coy Training. Digging party of 100 to SUTTON VENY. B Coy inspected by C.O.	F.R.R.
	16	Coy Training. C Coy inspected by C.O.	
	17	Coy Training. Kit & Foot inspection.	
	18 a.m. 9.45	Church parades.	
	19	Preparing for overseas	any
	20	Preparing for overseas. D.o/k of 33 received	any
	21	Preparing for move overseas on 22nd inst.	

Confidential

WAR DIARY

of

the 2/15th Battn LONDON REGIMENT

from

22 June 1916 to 30 June 1916

(Volume 2)

Army Form C.2118

WAR DIARY
or
INTELLIGENCE SUMMARY
(Erase heading not required.)

Instructions regarding War Diaries and Intelligence Summaries are contained in F. S. Regs., Part II. and the Staff Manual respectively. Title Pages will be prepared in manuscript.

Place	Date	Hour	Summary of Events and Information	Remarks and references to Appendices
LONGBRIDGE DEVERILL	June 22	7.20 a.m	1st Half Battn. left camp with 16 men of 2/13th Battn. attached	
		8.20	2nd " " " " " "	
WARMINSTER		9	1st train left. Transport entrained in 18 mins. Battn. in 10 mins.	
		10.20	2nd train left.	
SOUTHAMPTON		11.30 a.m 12.30	Trains arrived at port of embarkation. One L.D. horse was exchanged	Aug.
		5	S.S. INVENTOR left with Transport	
		5.45	H.T. CONNAUGHT left with Battalion.	
HAVRE	23	1 a.m	H.T CONNAUGHT arrived. Voyage without mishap	
		1.45	S.S INVENTOR arrived	
		7 a.m	Battn. disentrained and proceeded to DOCKS REST CAMP. One case of measles and 4 cases of influenza to hospital. One horse drawn to complete establishment. 2 draught and 2 riding horses exchanged.	Aug
	24	4 am	25 Officers 741 Other ranks with transport left Camp and entrained at June 3.	
		7.40	Train left	
		1 pm	Halts at MONTEROLIER BUCHY	
		7.5	Halt at ABBEVILLE	
		11	Train arrived at PETIT HOUVIN. Battn. detrained and proceeded to	

1875 Wt. W593/326 1,000,000 4/15 J.B.C. & A. A.D.S.S./Forms/C. 2118.

WAR DIARY or INTELLIGENCE SUMMARY

Army Form C. 2118

Instructions regarding War Diaries and Intelligence Summaries are contained in F.S. Regs., Part II and the Staff Manual respectively. Title Pages will be prepared in manuscript.

(Erase heading not required.)

Place	Date	Hour	Summary of Events and Information	Remarks and references to Appendices
	25	7 am	BUNEVILLE and went into billets. Balance of Battn 6 officers and 250 other ranks left HAVRE. This party arrived	aux
PENIN		3 am	at ST POL and proceeded by march route to PENIN	aux
		2.10 pm	Battn less 6 officers and 250 other ranks. Proceeded by march route to PENIN	aux
MAROEUIL	26	6 pm	Battn proceeded by march route to MAROEUIL and went into billets	aux
	27	am	A further company proceeded to ECOIVRES	aux
		1.10	Enemy artillery fired 5 shells into billets destroying the billets of A Coy field kitchen and wounding two men. C.O. Batt major Adjt. and two Company Commanders visit troops Commander	aux
	28	5	Battn proceeded to BRAY HUTS	aux
	29	11 pm	LT F.J.SMITH and 11 other ranks left for Trench Mortar School	aux
		3 pm	Battn left for instruction in the Trenches A.C Coy officers R.O & T.Karshine Gazette LT.T.RIMINGTON to be captain 12.5.16 & 2nd LTS. F.W LEWIS, C.M KILNER A.V. JAMES and F.J.SMITH to be LIEUTENANTS 24.6.16	aux
	30	4 pm	Platoons of A and C Coys commenced instruction in firing line	aux

Appendix

Divisional Tactical Exercise May 26th, 1916.

179th Brigade

Operation Orders

by

Col E.W. Baird, Commanding.

DIVISIONAL EXERCISE.

179th Infantry Brigade. No. 1.

ORDERS

by

Colonel E.W.Baird, Commanding.

LONGBRIDGE DEVERILL.
26th May, 1916.

Ref:- Order Sur.Sheet 122. 1" to 1 Mile.

1. **ENEMY.** As in Divisional "Situation".

2. **INTENTION.** It is the intention of the G.O.C. to deliver a Frontal Attack with one Brigade and to turn the enemy's left with another.

3. **DIVISIONAL MOUNTED TROOPS.** Divisional Mounted Troops and Cyclists will be operation against enemy's left in the vicinity of SHERINGTON, CORTON and TYTHERINGTON HILL.

4. **ARTILLERY.** The Corps Artillery will bombard the enemy's position for an hour prior to the Infantry Attack paying particular attention to points 745 and 784. It will also establish a barrage of fire from 11 a.m. to 2.0 p.m. on the roads and tracks leading South from LONGBRIDGE DEVERILL, SUTTON VENY and TYTHERINGTON.
   The 301st Brigade, R.F.A. will support the frontal attack and 300th Brigade R.F.A. the turning movement.
   The remainder of the Artillery will be employed as C.R.A. directs.
   The Artillery will open fire at 10.30 a.m.

5. **INFANTRY AND R.E.** (a) 180th Infantry Brigade and 1/6th Company, R.E. will make a frontal attack between Cross Tracks by S of TUMULUS (inclusive) to EAST KNOYLE - WESTBURY Road (exclusive).
   (b) 179th Infantry Brigade and 2/4th Company R.E. will attack enemy's left flank on a front between wood at BRITISH VILLAGE (inclusive) to Cross Tracks mentioned in (a) inclusive.
   (c) 181st Infantry Brigade and 3/3rd Company, R.E. will be in Divisional Reserve.

6. **DISPOSITION.** (a) Firing Line. 2/13th and 2/16th Bn.,L.R.
   (b) Supports. 2/15th Bn., L.R. 500 yards in rear of Centre.
   (c) Reserves. 2/14th Bn., L.R. and 2/4th Company, R.E. Echeloned 500 yards in rear of right of supporting Battalion.
   Battalions will deploy in Artillery formation under cover of GREAT RIDGE Wood and will advance through the wood in that formation.
   Great care is to be taken on nearing the N. Edge of the wood that no man exposes himself. The leading Battalions on reaching a line 20 yards S. of the N. edge of the wood will halt and await orders to advance, the supports and reserves lying down in their respective positions in rear.
   The 2/13th Battalion will be the directing battalion and will advance with its left flank 20 yards inside W. Edge of Wood.

- 2 -

6. DISPOSITION.
   (Contd.).
The remaining Battalions and R.E. will make the necessary arrangements for retaining their relative positions.
On advancing from N. Edge of the wood the first objective will be to seize the REDDING HANGING Ridge from a point S. of G in REDDING to a point S. of N in LONG BOTTOM.
During this advance the O.C., 2/13th Bn., L.R. will get in touch with the left attack. During the further advance to the final objective the O.C. 2/16th Bn., L.R. will endeavour to push forward the right flank with the object of driving in the enemy's left.
When the final position is reached steps will at once be taken to consolidate it, six strips of trench 100 yards long being dug.

7. MEDICAL.
The O.C. 2/4th Field Ambulance will establish a Dressing Station under cover of S./. Corner of Great Ridge Wood.

8. REPORTS.
Reports to point of Wood S. of S in STARVHALL.

W.N.HERBERT.

MAJOR.
Brigade Major.
179th Infantry Brigade.

Issued at
O.C. 2/13th Bn.   6 copies.
    2/14th Bn.   6 copies.
    2/15th Bn.   6 copies.
    2/16th Bn.   6 Copies.
    R.E.   1 Copy.
    Fld. Ambce.   1 Copy.

60TH DIVISION
179TH INFY BDE.

2-15TH BN LONDON REGT

~~JUN — NOV 1916~~

1915 JAN — 1916 NOV

Vol II

Confidential

WAR DIARY

of

The 2/15th Battn London Regt.

from 1 July 1916 to 31 July 1916

(Volume 2.)

WAR DIARY
or
INTELLIGENCE SUMMARY
(Erase heading not required.)

Army Form C. 2118

Instructions regarding War Diaries and Intelligence Summaries are contained in F.S. Regs., Part II. and the Staff Manual respectively. Title Pages will be prepared in manuscript.

Place	Date	Hour	Summary of Events and Information	Remarks and references to Appendices
TRENCHES	July 1		No 3426 Pte W J WARD killed in action, 1850 Pte D M BYRNE C Co. 1543 Pte HINGSTON A wounded.	unf.
		6 p.m.	A and C Companies took over as companies in the firing line for 24 hours	
	2	6 p.m.	A and C Companies were relieved by 1/7 4th BLACK WATCH and went into reserve. B and D Companies went up into support line, and Officers and N.C.O's commenced instruction in front line. Lce Cpl C. CHEALE wounded.	unf.
		11 a.m.	O.R. Sgt. C.J. NEWMAN left to join D.A.G.'s Office 3rd ECHELON vice Sgt POSTLE OR clerk.	
		7 a.m.	LIEUT A.V. TAMES and two other ranks left for a GAS COURSE at ST POL.	
	3	6 p.m.	B/D company platoons go into front line for instruction. No 2248 Pte F.C. HUSSEY and No. 2248 L/Cpl BENDLE H.C. wounded. do to	unf.
	4	6 "	B and D Companies took over front line positions for 24 hours. No 3464 Pte H.S. WOOD, and No 1816 Pte R.C. PICKERING wounded.	unf.
	5	2 p.m.	2nd LT F W WESTMORE to hospital HAEMORRHOIDS	unf.
NEUVILLE ST VAST		4 p.m.	BATTN commenced being relieved, and proceeded to NEUVILLE ST VAST. Relief was greatly hampered by weather, and trench mortar bombardment by an O.C. DEFENCES, and the 2/13 4th BATTN at NEUVILLE. 1/2 Co lathing over duty last lalution did not arrive until 2 a.m. No 5057 Pte BRANGWIN L.M.L accidentally wounded, and No 3297 Pte C BOWDEN wounded working parties for R.E's	unf.

WAR DIARY
or
INTELLIGENCE SUMMARY
(Erase heading not required.)

Army Form C. 2118.

Place	Date	Hour	Summary of Events and Information	Remarks and references to Appendices
NEUVILLE ST VAAST	July 6	9 am	CAPT CHRIMINGTON, 2nd LTS. H.J. SPENCER, E.E. ANDREWS, and C.E. THOMPSON with 2 NCO's and 4 Batmen left for GRENADE COURSE at HERMAVILLE.	any.
	7		CAPTAIN K.W.M. PICKTHORN and Lce Sgt A.S. CHARLTON proceeded to details to join 3rd ARMY SCHOOL at AUXI LE CHATEAU on the 9th.	any
	8		No 4388 Pte H.A. PARKINS A Coy and No 3260 Pte C.J. PIKE A Coy wounded when on working party. Lce Cpt A.J. CLIVE returned from 17th BRIGADE and No 4975 Pte H. STRINGER A Coy taken on Regdl strength replacing above. any	any
	9		CAPTAIN A.G.H. BENKE sent to 1/2 HIGHLAND FIELD AMBULANCE.	any.
	10		Nothing of interest. Orders received that BATTN. would be relieved on the night of the 12/13th inst.	any.
	11		C.O. Majors of 1/6 th CORDON. HIGHLANDERS arrived to make arrangements for relief. 2nd LIEUT. WESTMORE returned from hospital.	any.
			Proceed on	any.

WAR DIARY
or
INTELLIGENCE SUMMARY

(Erase heading not required.)

Army Form C. 2

Place	Date	Hour	Summary of Events and Information	Remarks and references to Appendices
NEUVILLE ST. VAST	July 12	8 pm	Lewis Gun Relief completed. Parties of 1/6th CORDONS arrived to take over right working parties	aug
		11 pm	First company left.	
	13	12.30 am	Relief completed without casualties.	aug
		1.25	First company arrived in BRAY HUTS	
		2.30	Last company arrived	
BRAY.				
	14	6 am	C. Coy proceeded to Trenches in BRIGADE support at RHINE SHELTERS. Salvage party 5 other ranks left for MAROEUIL to work for DIV. SALVAGE CORPS. Notice received of Dolphin & 40 other ranks reinforcements. Courses held in Lewis Gun, Bombing, Sniping, Gas Intelligence, Company instructions by S.O. in evening. 3 other ranks left behind in hospital at HAVRE rejoined. A Funeral of 2 Pts and 20 O.R. furnished for TOWN MAJOR at MAROEUIL. Orders received to relieve 2/14 Battn in Trenches!. on 15th.	aug
	15	11 am	LEWIS GUN Section left to trenches, followed by the Batten at 2 pm	aug
		2 pm	Relief completed without casualties. Detachments fromKILNER & ST POL for gas course; 2 men to BDE for SALVAGE on cyclist orderly to Division	
		2.5		
	16		Line extended 50 yds N. S. taking over from 18/st BRIGADE. C/W HUTHWAITE D Coy wounded	aug

Army Form C. 2118.

WAR DIARY
or
INTELLIGENCE SUMMARY
(Erase heading not required.)

Place	Date	Hour	Summary of Events and Information	Remarks and references to Appendices
SUBSECTOR I	July 17	a.m. 12.10 12.40	Enemy opened heavy bombardment on right and left centre, with trench mortars, heavy. Retaliation obtained from artillery with good result. Nos 6038 Pte BERRY A.V. and 6015 Pte COCKROFT J.W. killed. 3 other ranks wounded. CAPT A.C.H. BENKÉ rejoined from hospital. 2nd Lts MARTIN and PEARSON re-inforcements reported for duty.	aw.g
	18		Pte COLLINS A. N. 6090 died of wounds. No 6024 Pte VANDERSLUIS W. killed and 4 other ranks wounded. by shell. No 4412 Pte MARSHALL G.Y. died of wounds.	aw.g
	19	2 a.m.	No 4354 Pte HARRIS. E. killed in action. 7 other ranks wounded during trench Mortar bombardment in early morning. 2nd Lts MARTIN and PEARSON to Divl GAS SCHOOL. Relief of Battn commenced. Heavy trench mortar bombardment delayed relief.	aw.g
		5.35	Relief completed without casualties. Dispositions A.C. right and left supports. B Coy Reserve. D coy support for two subsectors. Headquarters moved to MAISON BLANCHE. CAPT. K.A. WILLS attached to 179 Bde HQ.	Ply J.
	20 21		5927 Pte R. EASTER D Coy killed in action. 2 other ranks wounded. CPL FITZGERALD and 3 drummers sent to MARŒUIL as permanent working party R.E. 2907 Pte B PERCIVAL - B to 3rd Army 3rd Field Survey Co.	Ply J. Ply J.
	22		2nd LT MARTIN & 2 LT PEARSON rejoined from Gas Course ACQ	Ply J.

Army Form C. 2118

WAR DIARY
or
INTELLIGENCE SUMMARY
(Erase heading not required.)

Place	Date	Hour	Summary of Events and Information	Remarks and references to Appendices
SUBSECTOR	July 23		Four N.C.O's to Divisional Physical Training Course. No 59936 Pte. J. BALLANTINE to THIRD ARMY as Clerk to A.M.S.	AWF.
	24		2nd Lt. H.J. SPENCER and 2nd Lt. L.H. HART to Physical Training Course.	AWF
	25		Nothing of interest. The Company in support in Subsectors 2 were called upon to stand to, but nothing resulted.	AWF
	26		CAPTAIN F.R. RADICE granted 8 days leave by G.O.C. XVII CORPS. CAPT A.C.H. BENKÉ assumed command of D Coy.	AWF.
	27		The Battn. relieved the 2/14th Battn. in the firing line. New dispositions were made, the firing line being taken over by 3 companies instead of 4. Final disposition, A.C.D Companies firing line, B Coy Left-support. Rifle support and Reserve Company furnished by the 2/13th 4 Battn. The relief was completed at 2 A.m. without casualties. 2nd Lt. A.V. JAMES admitted to No 6 STATIONARY HOSPITAL. No 5048 Pte NEWELL F. died of wounds.	AWF
	28			
	29		Two GERMANS taken by A Coy. Proved to belong to 184th Regt. The men were handed over to the BRIGADE.	AWF
	30		No. 2865 Pte J. GABRIEL killed in action. 3 men wounded. A patrol of C Coy went out & discovered the body of a German patrol	AWF

Army Form C. 2118

WAR DIARY
or
INTELLIGENCE SUMMARY
(Erase heading not required.)

Instructions regarding War Diaries and Intelligence Summaries are contained in F.S. Regs., Part II. and the Staff Manual respectively. Title Pages will be prepared in manuscript.

Place	Date	Hour	Summary of Events and Information	Remarks and references to Appendices
SUBSECTOR 1	30		Thought to have been shot the previous night. His helmet was obtained and confirmed the fact that the 184th Regt. was in front.	appx
	31		B Coy relieved C Coy in the front line that Relief completed 10 am without casualties. No. 5235 Pte J.W. THOMAS A Coy. killed in action 3 men wounded. 2nd Lt. E.F. ANDREWS and 6 other ranks left for Div. Trench Mortar School.	appx

C. Dickson Lt. Col
2/15th Battn. LOND REGT.

2/15 London Vol II

Confidential

WAR DIARY

of

The 2/15th. Battn London Regiment

from

1 August 1916 to 31 August 1916

(Volume 2)

Army Form C.

WAR DIARY
or
INTELLIGENCE SUMMARY
(Erase heading not required.)

Instructions regarding War Diaries and Intelligence Summaries are contained in F. S. Regs., Part II. and the Staff Manual respectively. Title Pages will be prepared in manuscript.

Place	Date	Hour	Summary of Events and Information	Remarks and references to Appendices
SUBSECTOR H	Aug 1		Situation normal. No casualties	aug
	2		No 5221 Pte J. KILBY C Coy killed in action on Enemy Patrol. 3 P. B.O's wounded in A Coy, including the B. Coy S.M.	aug
	3		No 1797 L/C P.E. STEVENS A Coy killed in action. 3 men wounded.	aug
	4	4.30 a.m.	The relief of the Battn by the 2/14 th Battn commenced, the relief proceeded without mishap and was completed in 1½ hours.	aug
		7	H.Q moved to BRAY for eight day's rest.	
	5		In rest billets, men engaged in bathing and refitting. Funeral of 20 other ranks	aug
	6		furnished for Town Major MAROEUIL. Church Parades. 2nd LTS. H.T.G BACK and C.F. CLEGG joined for duty from 3rd Line	aug
	7		via Base Camp HAVRE. In rest Billets. Notification received that 2nd LT WESTMORE was invalided to ENGLAND on the 1st of August.	aug
	8		No 3416 Pte PRIDEAUX H.L. accidentally wounded during LEWIS GUN instruction. L/CPL LLOYD placed under arrest, and Court of Inquiry held.	aug
	9		In rest billets. H.M the KING passed through the Battn was present on the line of route. 2nd LT H.T.G. BACK to Duct Gas School.	aug

1875 Wt. W593/826 1,000,000 4/15. J.B.C. & A. A.D.S.S/Forms/C. 2118.

Army Form C. 2118

WAR DIARY
or
INTELLIGENCE SUMMARY
(Erase heading not required.)

Instructions regarding War Diaries and Intelligence Summaries are contained in F.S. Regs., Part II. and the Staff Manual respectively. Title Pages will be prepared in manuscript.

Place	Date	Hour	Summary of Events and Information	Remarks and references to Appendices
REST BILLETS	AUG 10		In rest billets	aug.
"	11		In rest billets	aug.
	12	2 pm	Battn. left billets en route for the trenches to relieve 2/14th Battn.	aug.
		6.40	Relief completed without casualties. Disposition B Coy. Rgt. C Centre. D Left. A right support.	aug.
	13		No 5084 Pte G. A. BOLTON D Co. wounded on 12th inst died of wounds in hospital. LT. P. W. THOROGOOD to 2/4th Field Ambulance. Finish fever. Field General Court martial on 7/Cpl. F.S. LLOYD for an act to the prejudice etc in wearing a hair wound, unhurt lt oedema, when motorcycling in the Lewis Gun. Proceedings. Prisoner's Friend LT. PEATFIELD. Prisoner's Friend LT. W.S.H. SMITH	aug.
	14		Enemy activity nil & trench mortars. No 5026 Pte TOLHURST G.H. killed in action, two men wounded	aug.
	15		Normal day. Casualties nil	aug.
	16		A Boy relieved. D coy in left bombing front line Draft of 40 men arrived at Rear H.Q. No casualties. Rain heavy 2½ hours late, came to within a hundred at rear.	aug.
	17	6 pm	38 of the Draft arrived for duty. 5 men attached to Lyte T.M. Battery. Artillery activity on enemy frontier immediately N of Left Company	aug.

Army Form C. 2118

WAR DIARY
or
INTELLIGENCE SUMMARY
(Erase heading not required.)

Instructions regarding War Diaries and Intelligence Summaries are contained in F. S. Regs., Part II. and the Staff Manual respectively. Title Pages will be prepared in manuscript.

Place	Date	Hour	Summary of Events and Information	Remarks and references to Appendices
2nd Sub Sector 1	Aug 18	5	Situation normal. Enemy activity very small. No casualties for men attached to	appx
	19		62 X 2" T.M Battery. Orders received for relief on 20". Two suspicious men in R.E. signal section uniform found to belong to one of the R.B. Batteries, and sent under escort. Nothing of interest.	appx
	20	4 am	Battn. relieved in the front line by the 2/14 M Battn. Relief completed without casualties. Disposition after relief B. A Coy Support and Reserve Sub Section I. C & D Support and Reserve Sub Sector 2. LT P.W THOROGOOD rejoined from hospital.	appx
	21		2nd LT L.H HART to hospital 2nd LT E.E. ANDREWS and 4 N.C.O.'s to physical training course. Court of Enquiry held at H.Q on accidental wounding of No 2253 Pte BEER R.G. by No Cpl. KA SEVILLE at Room H.Q.	appx
	22		2T. PEATFIELD 12nd LT. THOMPSON and 46 other ranks proceeded to Bn. H.Q for special course in trench fighting.	appx
	23		2nd LT. A.D. LANE reported for duty from Base Camp. CAPT F.R. RADICE proceeded to Dn H.Q to take charge of GERMAN Prisoners	appx
	24		Situation normal.	appx
	25		Situation normal. A hostile aeroplane was hit in the proximity of MAISON BLANCHE but	appx

WAR DIARY
or
INTELLIGENCE SUMMARY
(Erase heading not required.)

Army Form C. 2118

Instructions regarding War Diaries and Intelligence Summaries are contained in F.S. Regs., Part II. and the Staff Manual respectively. Title Pages will be prepared in manuscript.

Place	Date	Hour	Summary of Events and Information	Remarks and references to Appendices
September 1	Sept 26	7 p.m.	Battn relieved 2/14th Battn in front line. Disposition. A Coy Right, B Coy Centre, D Coy Left. C Coy Right Support. Relief completed without casualties. No. 1431 Pte B M CHAPMAN killed in action. 2nd Lt PEARSON and 4 N.C.O.'s to Brebis. Consolidation normal.	aug
	27		2nd LTSS A TAYLOR and F.W. PHELPS and draft of 13 men joined for duty	aug
	28		2285 2/Cpl K A SEVILLE tried by F.G.C.M. for refusing orders on sentry. Prosecutor Capt. K A WILLS	aug
	28		Situation normal.	aug
	29		Decision F.G.C.M on 2/Cpl SEVILLE received. Sentence 30 days F P No 1.	aug
	30		Above sentence promulgated. Battn Consolidation former party returned. 2nd LTS L.F. NEWTON F.H. Du HEAUME, R.B.W.G. ANDREW, L.E.C. CRIBBETT, and T.H ARUNDEL joined for duty from Reserve Battn.	aug
	31		Pte F.S. SAUNDERS killed in action, and 3 men wounded	aug

I. O. S ///1012
Lt. Col.
cdg. 2/15th Battn LONDON REGIMENT

Vol 4

179/60

Confidential

War Diary
of
2/15th London Regt. from
1 Sept 1916 to 30 Sept 1916.

(Volume 2)

Army Form C. 2118

WAR DIARY
or
INTELLIGENCE SUMMARY
(Erase heading not required.)

Instructions regarding War Diaries and Intelligence Summaries are contained in F.S. Regs, Part II. and the Staff Manual respectively. Title Pages will be prepared in manuscript.

Place	Date	Hour	Summary of Events and Information	Remarks and references to Appendices
Sub Section I	Sept 1	am 7.20	Battn. was relieved in the front line trenches by the 2/14th Battn. and proceeded to Rest	
REST BILLETS			Billets. Relief completed without casualties. Refitting commenced	aug
"	2		Bathing and refitting. Party return from special course at Divl. Bomade School	aug
"	3		Church Parade. 2nd Lt. E. DENNY to report from duty from Rouen Battn, and posted to D Coy. 2nd Lt. S.A. TAYLOR and one N.C.O. per Coy. to Divl. Gas School. 2nd Lt. L.H. HART rejoined from Hospital.	aug
"	4		Draft of 60 other ranks joined for duty. The draft were of good physique and contained several men who had seen service overseas with the 1st BATTN. Training and digging bombing ground	aug
"	5		Training and digging bombing ground	aug
"	6		Training and preparing to move into Trenches	aug
"	7		The Battn relieved the 2/14th Battn. in the front line. Distribution A Coy. Right. C Coy. Centre. D Coy. Left. B Coy Right Support. a mine had been blown by the Enemy at 10 p.m. the previous night in Left Coy Front, and consolidation of crater was proceeded with at once. CAPT. K.W.M. PICKTHORN accidentally wounded by bayonet. No 2986 Pte. RULE A.C. died of wounds. One man wounded. 2nd Lt. P.G. HUTTON joined for duty and posted to B Coy	aug
"	8		Battalion normal, good trooper moved with consolidating new crater	aug

Army Form C. 2118

WAR DIARY
or
INTELLIGENCE SUMMARY
(Erase heading not required.)

Instructions regarding War Diaries and Intelligence Summaries are contained in F. S. Regs., Part II. and the Staff Manual respectively. Title Pages will be prepared in manuscript.

Place	Date	Hour	Summary of Events and Information	Remarks and references to Appendices
SUBSECTOR CENTRE 1	9		Situation normal. 2nd LT F. MARTIN to hospital. Trench fever.	enq
"	10		Situation normal, except for hostile artillery activity in Reserve Line. H.Q. Officers dug out entrance wrecked by shell.	enq
"	11	3 am	A raid was carried out on the enemy's trenches by a party of 40 other ranks under LIEUT. B. PEATFIELD and 2nd LIEUT. C.E. THOMPSON. 4 live prisoners were obtained one being wounded. Our losses No 3175 Pte SMALL T.F. killed. The two officers were wounded and slightly + 4 other ranks slightly. Congratulations were received from G.O.C. FIRST ARMY.	enq Appx. I + II
"	12		Situation normal. CAPTAIN K.W. PICKTHORN discharged from hospital & 5 days light duty.	enq
"	13	9 am	The Battn. was relieved from the firing line by the 2/14th Battn. and went into Support and Reserve. A. D. Coys R.+L. Coy supplied first Relief in Z.B.C. Support and Reserve respectively in Sub Sector 2.	enq
			2nd LIEUTS E.C.A MILES, H.H. SIMPSON and W.C.Y. MORTON joined for duty from Reserve Battalion. Nos 5146 Pte HISCOX W.V.C, 4693 IRWIN W.E. 4885 DAVIES S.T.R. killed in action when employed on a working party in the front line. No 2294 Pte LAKE ER ¼ Coy. charged with sleeping on his post on the morning of the 11th of Sept. remanded for F.C.C.M.	enq
	14		Battalion normal. LT P.W. THOROGOOD to 2/4th LON FIELD AMBULANCE	enq

WAR DIARY
or
INTELLIGENCE SUMMARY
(Erase heading not required.)

Army Form C. 2118

Instructions regarding War Diaries and Intelligence Summaries are contained in F.S. Regs., Part II. and the Staff Manual respectively. Title Pages will be prepared in manuscript.

Place	Date	Hour	Summary of Events and Information	Remarks and references to Appendices
SUBSECTOR CENTRE	SEPT 15		Situation normal. Information received by wire that Military Medal had been awarded to No 2271 SGT T.I. JONES, No 3382 PTE H.A. PLASTOW and No 4594 PTE A SMALL for gallant conduct during raid on the enemy trenches on the 11th of September.	See appendix III
	16		Situation normal	awg
	17		MAJOR H.F.M. WARNE and 2nd LT C.M. KILNER proceeded to 3rd ARMY SCHOOL OF INSTRUCTION	awg
	18		Situation normal	awg
	19		The Battn relieved the 2/1st Battn in the front line trenches. Disposition A Coy right, C Coy centre, B Coy left. D Coy Reserve. Relief completed by 6.15am. without casualties. —	awg
	20		Situation normal. Field General Court Martial on on PTE ER LAKE A Coy for sleeping on his post. Accused was found "not guilty." 2nd LTS HJG BACK and E DENNY to École Bomochalair Tourse. 2nd LIEUT. S.G. BENNET to hospital LT B PEATFIELD awarded Military Cross. 2nd LT G.E. THOMPSON awarded D.S.O. as result of the raid of 11th	See appendix IV
	21		2nd LTS F.W. PHELPS, F.H. DuHEAUME and 10 other ranks to Lewis Gun Course ETAPLES. One man died of wounds. Draft of two received from BASE DEPOT.	awg
	23		2265 ARC HAYWARD (L-CPL) to Musketry Course CAMIERS. CPL G.V. KNIGHT KILLED IN ACTION. PTE G.F. SHELTON died of wounds. Draft of 7 from BASE DEPOT	awg
	24		Situation normal	awg

Army Form C.2118

WAR DIARY
or
INTELLIGENCE SUMMARY
(Erase heading not required.)

Instructions regarding War Diaries and Intelligence Summaries are contained in F.S. Regs., Part II. and the Staff Manual respectively. Title Pages will be prepared in manuscript.

Place	Date	Hour	Summary of Events and Information	Remarks and references to Appendices
REST	25		BN relieved by 2/14 BN. LON. REGT.	P/S J
	26		CAPT A.W. GAZE proceeded on 10 days leave to ENGLAND. Promotion of hobby ranks by the Corps Commander to SGT JONES, PTE. SNALL, PTE. PLASTON.	P.W. J.
BILLETS	27		Inspection by LIEUT GENERAL SIR CHARLES FERGUSSON. The highest possible commendation was given. LT. THOROGOOD acting adjutant vice CAPT GAZE. PTE HONOUR awarded for F.G.C.M.	P.W. J.
	28		2/LT ECA MILES and 4 NCOS to cadets instruction course. PTE CONNETT died of wounds. Have received that 2/LT G.E. THOMPSON was invalided to ENGLAND on the 15th Sept. Draft of 2	P.W. J.
	29		Draft of 6 arrived from BASE DEPOT.	P.W. J.
	30		2nd LT. F.W. HOUNSELL joined for duty from BASE DEPOT.	

Archibald. Major
T.
for Lieut Col
Cdg 2/15th London Regt.

Appendix I

C O P Y.

G.O.C. XVII CORPS.

    I should be glad if you will direct the G.O.C. 60th Division to convey to Br.-General BAIRD, Commanding 179th Brigade, my thanks and appreciation of the action of the 2/15th Battalion London Regiment, under the command of Lt.-Colonel de PUTRON, last night, in carrying out their successful raid into the German trenches.

    The identification they obtained by the capture of prisoners is of exceptional value at the present time, and this information will be of the greatest service, not only to the British Army, but to the Armies of all the Allies who are fighting in different theatres of the War.

(Signed) R. H A K I N G
General
Cmmdg. 1st Army.

11/9/16.

Appendix II

Statement by Lieut. B. PEATFIELD.

The night previous to the raid was quiet. A German working party of approximately five men had been heard from 10 p.m. to midnight at work on the wire. Lewis gun fire was brought to bear on this party but their work was continued inside the German trenches.

At 2-15 a.m. Lieutenant Peatfield and 2nd Lieut. Thompson carried out the impedimenta, ladders and blankets, etc., to the head of the sap at point of departure.

At 2-30 a.m. the men were lined up in the sap.

At 2-45 a.m. the head of the party left the sap and crawled out toward a point in the German line previously selected and noted by compass bearing, 150 degrees magnetic.

Although the moon was obscured by cloud, a sniper fired upon the party on leaving the sap and bombs were thrown from the North but no damage was done. The head of the party reached the cover of thistles about 15 yards from the German wire and there awaited our Artillery fire.

The first salvo was fired at 3 a.m. whereupon the party rose up and walked to the wire.

The German wire was damaged but not wholly cut and the ground about the wire was cut up by shell holes.

The wire was 12 to 15 yards in depth and was successfully crossed by blanket bridges.

The bombing party entered the trench and proceeded to block it in accordance with the previously arranged programme.

The centre party found a German dugout at point of entry. 2nd Lieut. Thompson threw a bomb down the dugout, wounding some of the occupants, who were ordered in German to come out, with a threat that further bombs would be thrown. They obeyed and prisoners were taken and escorted back to our lines.

The party was in the German trenches about ten minutes.

The morale of the prisoners was exceedingly low, and they were so terrified that it was only with great difficulty they could be induced to come out of their trench.

The party was recalled at point of entry by code word, and retired in good order, bringing one of our party, who was wounded and helpless.

Much time was lost in getting both German and our wounded out of the trenches, and again crossing the wire with the casualties on the return journey. When the whole party had successfully evacuated the German trench, I handed over command to 2nd Lieut. Thompson as I felt weak from loss of blood, and feared I might have to be carried back.

In all four prisoners were taken, two of whom were I think wounded.

(1)

The Artillery fire was accurate and effective.

A further report from 2nd Lieut. Thompson will follow.

During the raid 2nd Lieut. Thompson acted with the greatest coolness and courage. The success of the raid in a great measure is due to his work.

The conduct of the men left nothing to be desired.

The Germans manned a little trench running South from point of entry immediately behind the main trench, and it was from this point that the bombs were thrown.

I laid a paper chase trail when going out which was extremely useful on the return journey.

11/9/1916.

Statement by 2nd Lieut. THOMPSON

We went over and met with absolutely no opposition till we were in the German trench, except from one sniper.

We were absolutely unopposed going over, except for one man in the trench, who they got out at once.

Corporal Jones's party ran on then and went up and blocked the left sap, but I stuck to the dugout just were we entered the trench.

The next thing was I stood at the dugout door and ordered them to come out. I kept on shouting .... and I caught two of them coming out, whom I passed back to the man behind me, but whom it was I could not say, though I don't know about the dugout on the left.

The next thing was I sent to Mr Peatfield if we should send the word "retire".

As I got the word passed along I went to the bottom of the steps where I met the fellows and got them to report when all were in. They climbed up the ladders and got out.

The last party to come out was Corporal Jones's party, and two of them got left.

Corporal Jones came running back to me to say he had a badly wounded man, and I immediately went back and we shouted to some of the men to help him up the ladder.

We stood and bombed the trenches left and right while they were being got up. At any rate we got them up, and the man that was hit on the ladder. I got another man to help.

Both the covering party as well as the bombers were got back.

Nobody else was hit and we got together a little covering party.

Corporal Jones, Sergeant Quinton and Corporal Blick stayed behind, and it took them a considerable time to get them down to the sap. We held the sap head until I got the word passed up that the final party had got into the dugout.

Then I called in the covering party and got them into the Paris Redoubt and got them all down into the dugout somehow, after which I crawled down myself. It was some time before I could make sure that everybody was in.

11/9/1916.

Appendix III

EXTRACT FROM 60TH DIVISIONAL ORDERS
dated 15th September, 1916.

No. 2271. Corporal THOMAS IDWAL JONES   -   MILITARY MEDAL.
Date of Award, 15th September, 1916.

    Formed one of a party which raided the enemy Trenches on the 11th September, 1916. He displayed great coolness and courage in handling his party and his example did much to ensure success.

No. 3382 Pte. HARRY A. PLASTOW   -   MILITARY MEDAL.
Date of Award, 15th September, 1916.

    Acted as leader of a blocking party in a raid on the enemy Trenches on the 11th September, 1916. He showed much courage and power of organisation, was the first to enter the hostile Trenches, and captured the first prisoner by jumping on a sentry and clubbing him.

    He subsequently formed one of a covering party to protect the retirement of wounded men.

No. 4594 Pte. ALEXANDER SMALL   -   MILITARY MEDAL.
Date of Award, 15th September, 1916.

    Formed one of the party which raided the enemy Trenches on 11th September, 1916. He did gallant work, and, after being wounded himself, returned to rescue and bring into our lines his brother who was mortally wounded in the raid.

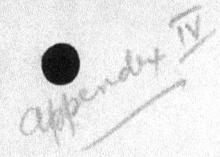

EXTRACT FROM 60TH DIVISIONAL ORDERS
dated 21st Sept. 1916.

para. 971.

HONOURS AND AWARDS.

2nd Lieut. GEORGE EDWARD THOMPSON - DISTINGUISHED SERVICE ORDER.

Date of Award - 21st September 1916.

Performed most gallant service in leading the bombers in a raid on the enemy trenches on the morning of 11th Sept., 1916. Although bleeding profusely from wounds he continued to fight and shot two Germans. He then helped a wounded man back to our lines and on arrival hearing that another Officer was missing, insisted on returning to search "No Man's Land".

He would not allow his wounds to be dressed, until he had ascertained that all the party had returned to our lines.

Lieut. BERNARD PEATFIELD - MILITARY CROSS.

Date of award - 21st September, 1916.

Led a raiding party on the enemy trenches on the morning of 11th Sept., 1916. He displayed great courage and gallantry, and although wounded at the outset, remained on the German parapet directing operations until the raid terminated. He then assisted to rescue a wounded man of his party.

The success of the raid was largely due to his efforts in organising and training the party.

Confidential

Vol 5

WAR DIARY

of

2/15th Battn. LONDON REGIMENT

from 1 Oct. 1916 to 31 Oct. 1916

(Volume 2)

WAR DIARY
or
INTELLIGENCE SUMMARY
(Erase heading not required.)

Army Form C. 2118

Instructions regarding War Diaries and Intelligence Summaries are contained in F.S. Regs., Part II. and the Staff Manual respectively. Title Pages will be prepared in manuscript.

Place	Date 1916	Hour	Summary of Events and Information	Remarks and references to Appendices
SUBSECTOR Centre I	Oct 1	7.30 am	Relieved the 2/14th Bn in No 1 Sub-Sector without sustaining casualties. A Co on the right, B company centre, D coy right, 2nd LT PHELPS and 2nd LT DUHBAUME rejoined from CORPS COMMANDER and BRIG-GENERAL on the recent inspection. (See Appendix)	App J
	2		2nd LT MILES rejoined from Crater Consolidation Course. Situation normal.	App J
	3		Situation normal.	
	4		Very heavy enemy gun & trench mortar trench fire. 2nd LT ARUNDEL and 4 NCO's returned from CRATER Course	aug
	5		CAPT and ADJT. A.W. GAZE returned to duty from special leave. Heavy enemy bombardment from trench mortars. Coy out in Right Coy's line down in following casualties. Cpt WICNEY PTE PUGSLEY and PTE STAFFORD. killed 8 PL. BORDER PTES, COWHERD and CALDER missing (untraced) Lwin PTES WHITING A Coy and ATKINS B Coy killed 4 men wounded. Shelling continued and much damage done to Right Coy's front line	aug
	6		heavy enemy activity. 2nd LT. CRIBBET and 4 N.T.O.s to Berlin Consolidation Course. No H.W. LEWIS A Coy wounded by accidental explosion of a bomb.	aug
	7		The Battn was relieved by the 2/16th Battn and went into support and reserve A Coy and support, D Coy left support trench 1 B Coy support and C Coy Reserve trench 2.	aug
	8	5 am	Being completed without casualties	aug
	9		Nothing of interest	aug
			Nothing of interest. situation normal.	aug

WAR DIARY
or
INTELLIGENCE SUMMARY
(Erase heading not required.)

Army Form C. 2118

Place	Date	Hour	Summary of Events and Information	Remarks and references to Appendices
SUBSECTOR I CENTRE SECTOR.	Oct 10		Situation normal.	aug
	11		No 5016 Pte K L MINTER B Coy killed in action. Two men wounded. Short casualties occurred in support line Pastula 2 during bombardment by enemy forwarding to a raid which was repulsed. Found by enquiry held an accidental wounding of Pte LEWIS. LT. COL DE PUTRON proceeded on leave to ENGLAND MAJOR. A. A. OLIVER took over command.	aug
	12		Situation normal.	aug
	13	6 am – 8 am	The Battalion relieved the 2/14 Batt in the front-line trenches. Relief completed without casualties. Positions B Coy RIGHT, C Coy CENTRE, D Coy LEFT A Coy Reserve.	aug
	14		2nd LT A D LANE and 4 NCO's proceeded on a Lewis Gun School Course.	aug
	15		CAPT A CH BENKE, LT H F RUST, and 2 Lt 20's left for a month's course at the 3rd Army School of Instruction. Field General Court Martial held on No 5693 Pte EDMUNDS B Coy "disobeying an lawful order of a superior officer". Prosecutor CAPTAIN TARVER. Prisoners friend LT H T RANDOLPH. 2nd LT A C THOMPSON and draft of 50 men joined from Base. Draft obtained at Rwn H.Q.	aug
	16		Combined bombardment of enemy lines by Heavy Artillery, Div Artillery and Trench Mortars. Own heavy mortar used.	aug

WAR DIARY
or
INTELLIGENCE SUMMARY
(Erase heading not required.)

Army Form C. 2118

Instructions regarding War Diaries and Intelligence Summaries are contained in F. S. Regs., Part II. and the Staff Manual respectively. Title Pages will be prepared in manuscript.

Place	Date	Hour	Summary of Events and Information	Remarks and references to Appendices
CENTRE SUBSECTOR	Oct. 17	9.30	Continued activity of enemy trench mortars. Left Front Company's dug out was blown in, Inmates dug out uninjured. Drafts of 30 other ranks arrived	awg
	18	7 pm	Enemy trench mortars bombarded outpost line for 30 minutes. Unusually quiet.	awg
Rest Billets	19	7 am	The Battn. was relieved by the 2/14th Battn. and proceeded to Rest Billets. LT. COL. C. DE PUTRON rejoined from leave	awg
"	20		In Rest Billets. Box Respirators Small issued to the Battn.	awg
"	21		Refitting and bathing. CAPTAIN. C. A BAILY returned from hospital	awg
"	22		Church Parades. Orders received to move to HERMAVILLE on 23rd Oct. on relief of 3rd CANADIAN DIVN.	awg
HERMAVILLE – TILLOY	23	1.30 pm	Battn. proceeded by march route to HERMAVILLE, was accommodated in huts. C¹D¹&½ and LEWIS GUNS were billeted at TILLOY.	awg
SÉRICOURT + HONVAL	24	8 am 9.30 2.15	Battn. left for new area, proceeding by IZEL-LES-HAMEAUX, VILLERS-SIRE-SIMON,-MAGNICOURT, HOUVIN & SÉRICOURT. B¹D¹ Companies were billeted in HONVAL. 2nd LT TAYLOR admitted to hospital	awg
"	25		In Billets. Training interfered with by rain	awg

WAR DIARY or INTELLIGENCE SUMMARY

Army Form C. 2118

Place	Date	Hour	Summary of Events and Information	Remarks and references to Appendices
SERICOURT to HONVAL	26		In Billets. Captain F.R. RADICE rejoined from duty at Prisoners of War Camp XIII Corps.	aug
"	27		In Billets. Billeting Party proceeded to BEALCOURT. 2nd Lt ANDREW and 12 other ranks rejoined from LEWIS GUN SCHOOL.	aug
"	28	9.30 am / 2.30 pm	Battn. joined Brigade and proceeded by march route to BEALCOURT. A, B coys and H.Q. were billeted. C & D companies being at BEAUVOIR RIVIÈRE.	aug
BEALCOURT	29	9 am	Battn left billets and joined Brigade and proceeded by march route to LANCHES	aug
LANCHES	30	2 pm	where A, B coys and H.Q. were billeted. C coy at ST HILAIRE, D coy at BARLETTE. In Billets. Training	aug
"	31		In Billets. Training	aug

[signed] C.C. 2/15th London Regt.

Confidential

Vol 6

WAR DIARY

of

The 2/15th Battn. London Regt.

from 1 Nov. to 30 Nov. 1916

(Volume 2)

original

Army Form C.118

WAR DIARY
or
INTELLIGENCE SUMMARY
(Erase heading not required.)

Instructions regarding War Diaries and Intelligence Summaries are contained in F.S. Regs, Part II. and the Staff Manual respectively. Title Pages will be prepared in manuscript.

Place	Date	Hour	Summary of Events and Information	Remarks and references to Appendices
LANCHES	NOV 1		In Rest Billets. Training. The Battn was inspected by General SIR DOUGLAS HAIG Commander in Chief.	aug
	2		Instructions received to withdraw all Bombs. SAA ex wpt 120 rounds per man and 2000 rounds per first arrival. Orders received to move on following day. 2nd Lt. DENNY admitted to Hospital. 2nd LT. S.C. TAYLOR rejoined from Hospital.	aug
FRANCIÈRES	3	9.30 am 1.30	Battn proceeded by road route to FRANCIERES, joining Brigade at 10.50 am arrival. 2 LT. C.M. KILNER and 2nd LT. K.A. HIGGS admitted to Hospital.	aug
"	4		In Rest Billets. Training. Preliminary orders received to move Overseas, on establishments WAR EST Part XII	aug
"	5		Church Parade + Training.	aug
"	6		Seven G.S. limbered wagons + 18 horses handed over to 3rd Divn ASC MAJOR A.A. OLIVER CAPTAINS C.A. BAILY C.H. RIMINGTON LTS A.A. JOSLIN & W.S.H. SMITH, 2nd LT F.T. BAILEY proceeded to ENGLAND on leave with 8 other ranks.	aug
"	7		In Billets. Training.	aug
"	8		In Billets. Training. 2nd LT. F.W. LEWIS rejoined from Hospital	aug
"	9		Battn inspected by C.O.C. BRIG. GEN L.E.W. BAIRD who took leave of the Battn on giving up command of the Brigade	aug

WAR DIARY
or
INTELLIGENCE SUMMARY
(Erase heading not required.)

Army Form C.2118

Instructions regarding War Diaries and Intelligence Summaries are contained in F. S. Regs., Part II. and the Staff Manual respectively. Title Pages will be prepared in manuscript.

Place	Date	Hour	Summary of Events and Information	Remarks and references to Appendices
FRANCIERES	Nov 10		In Rest Billets	aux.g
"	11		In Rest Billets. Establishment on going overseas increased to 39 officers & 931 other ranks	aux.g
"	12		Church Parade. B.O. and Coy Officers on tactical exercise. Capt. BENKE, LT RUST & 6 other ranks returned from 3rd Army School. Officers on leave returned	aug
"	13		Orders for move received. Trained establishment 9 Officers 260 other ranks	aug.
"	14	4.m 3.40	Move commenced. MAJOR H.F.M WARNE. LT KILNER. 2nd LT KA HICCS. LT AV JAMES + 2nd LT DENNY HQ A Coy Transport. Lewis Gunners & 2nd LT THOMPSON + 41 O.R. handed to No. 7 I.B.D. LONGPRE	aug.
LONGPRE	15	4.m 2.30	Train twenty left by train. Spent 5 hours halt return to Platoon of preceding train and awaiting D.A.C. wagons	aug.
FRANCIERES		4.m 4.40 9.27 4.m 12.20 4.m 4.m 3.40	2nd twenty Infantry & 4 Officers left 3rd " C Coy details of A boy total 4 Officers 210 or 4th " D " " " 4 " 210 or 5th " B " Transport total 4 " 210 of	aug.
	16		On the train	
MARSEILLES	17	4.m 4	First twenty arrived at MARSEILLES and proceeded to CAMP CARCASSONNE.	aug
		4.m 6.30	hurried to CAMP FOURNIER	aug
	18	a.m 2	2nd Party arrived	aug
			3rd Party arrived	aug

WAR DIARY
or
INTELLIGENCE SUMMARY
(Erase heading not required.)

Army Form C. 2118

Instructions regarding War Diaries and Intelligence Summaries are contained in F.S. Regs., Part II. and the Staff Manual respectively. Title Pages will be prepared in manuscript.

Place	Date	Hour	Summary of Events and Information	Remarks and references to Appendices
MARSEILLES	Nov 18	4.20 am	4th Train arrived	aug
	19	10 am	5th Train arrived	aug
		11 am	B.D. Hqrs 20 officers and 365 other ranks embd. MAJOR A/A OLIVER embarked on H.T. TRANSYLVANIA which left the same evening	aug
	20		Remainder of Battn remained in camp	aug
	21		do	aug
	22	9 am	Balance of Battn less 1 Officer 20 other ranks, 24 horses embarked on board H.T. MECANTIC. Remainder on H.T. MENOMINEE. Lt Col de PUTRON o.c. Troops on both	aug
	23		Vessel commenced in port & left port before midnight	aug
	24		at sea	aug
	25		at sea	aug
	26		at sea	aug
	27		at sea	aug
	28	7.30 am	at sea Hostile submarine sighted astern submerged on arrival of escort	aug
SALONIKA	29	9 am	Arrived in anchorage at SALONIKA	aug
	30	12.30	Detachment disembarked and proceeded to USHANTA camp	aug
			Detachment from H.T. TRANSYLVANIA arrived in camp	aug

Aschwin. Major

www.ingramcontent.com/pod-product-compliance
Lightning Source LLC
Chambersburg PA
CBHW051527190426
43193CB00045BA/2225